FATHER ABRAHAM

Part Two: Patriarchal History

KEN FOOKES

Cover Photo

Abraham Casting Out Hagar and Ishmael (1657)
by Guercino

ISBN: 979-8-88615-210-4 (Paperback)

Inks and Bindings
888-290-5218
www.inksandbindings.com
orders@inksandbindings.com

PART TWO
PATRIARCHAL HISTORY

TABLE OF CONTENTS

INTRODUCTION TO THE PATRIARCHS

We have just finished the prehistory of the Bible. We have learned God created the universe and the earth. After creating the earth and filling it with all manner of plant and animal life, He then created men and women. Placing them in a beautiful garden and gave them dominion over the whole of the earth, but man failed God's test of obedience. The sin was of the flesh. The result of this failure was expulsion from the Garden of Eden, and no longer would we be able to just pick the fruit of the garden for sustenance; all of mankind would henceforth earn his way by the sweat of his brow.

Genesis 3:19

> In the sweat of thy face shalt thou eat bread, till thou return unto the ground; for out of it wast thou taken: for dust thou art, and unto dust shalt thou return.

And woman would bring forth children in pain.

Genesis 3:16

> Unto the woman he said, I will greatly multiply thy sorrow and thy conception; in sorrow thou shalt bring forth children; and thy desire shall be to thy husband, and he shall rule over thee.

Next, there is the murder of Abel by his brother Cain. Cain had pride in his labor and the fruit there of, but God required a blood offering, not a gain offering. When God rejected Cain's offering but accepted his brother Abel's, Cain was angry and jealous, which led to hatred for his brother and so he murdered him, because of the sin of pride. Satan also fell because of the sin of pride. Pride is the sin of the mind.[1]

Isaiah 14:12–15

> 12. How art thou fallen from heaven, O Lucifer, son of the morning! how art thou cut down to the ground, which didst weaken the nations!
> 13. For thou hast said in thine heart, I will ascend into heaven, I will exalt my throne above the stars of God: I will sit also upon the mount of the congregation, in the sides of the north:

---

[1] . J. Vernon McGee, *Thru the Bible*, page 56.

14. I will ascend above the heights of the clouds; I will be like the most High.
15. Yet thou shalt be brought down to hell, to the sides of the pit.

Humanity continued on a path of willful disobedience to God's commandments. They were obedient in one area for they multiplied on the earth, but their hearts were hardened, and there was cruelty and lust of the flesh. So after the death of Methuselah, being 969 years old, God commanded Noah to come into the Arc for He was about to bring judgment on all mankind, save Noah and his family. After the animals and Noah and his family were safely aboard the Arc, God shut them in and flooded the earth. The sinful nature and rebellious spirit of humankind was washed away.

For a while, humankind obeyed God, spreading across the landscape, until the man named Nimrod. Nimrod was a mighty hunter of men and convinced them to build a city and a great tower to make a name for themselves. God seeing this said enough and confused their tongues. Then and only then did men and women fanned out over the earth and replenished the earth. God no longer will deal with all of mankind, but individuals.

These first eleven chapters take in a period of 2000 years. The remainder of Genesis chapters (12–50) deals with the patriarchs and covers only 350 years. It is interesting to note the rest of the entire Bible covers a 2000 years' time.[2]

The patriarchs consist of just four men. The first being Abraham (Genesis 12–23), a man of faith and known as a friend of God:

2 Chronicles 20:7
> Art not thou our God, who didst drive out the inhabitants of this land before thy people Israel, and gavest it to the seed of Abraham thy friend for ever?

---

2   . J. Vernon McGee, *Thru the Bible*, page 56.

INITIATION OF THE COVENANT
Genesis 12

Abraham's Journey by József Molnár (1880)[3]

CHAPTER OVERVIEW

In this chapter of Genesis, we are introduced to Abram, "exalted father," and God will later change his name to Abraham, "father of many nations."

---

3   . http://freechristimages.org/biblestories/abrahams_journey.htm.

Genesis 17: 5

    Neither shall thy name any more be called Abram, but thy name shall be Abraham; for a father of many nations have I made thee.

Although he lived in a land that worshiped many gods, God, Yahweh called him to leave the place of his birth and his family and journey to land God would show him. Abram's father Terah worshiped idols according to

Joshua 24:2

    And Joshua said unto all the people, Thus saith the LORD God of Israel, Your fathers dwelt on the other side of the flood in old time, even Terah, the father of Abraham, and the father of Nachor: and they served other gods.

In accordance with Jewish tradition, he was an idol maker. Because God called Abram to come out of his father's house and travel to the land of Canaan would imply that he was not a worshiper of idols. At the time of his calling, Abram resided in the city of Ur of the Chaldees, which is located on Euphrates river in modern southeastern Iraq.

The city of Ur was believed to have been established about 4500 years ago, comparable to a large city of today. Archaeologists have found evidence of schools, public building, and have uncovered well-crafted jewelry. All of these finding would suggest Ur was a wealthy city. The citizens practiced pantheism or the worship of nature, and in the case of Ur, they worshiped deities of fire, sun, moon, and stars. Ur was a sinful city requiring their female citizens to be in the service of Ningal, the moon goddess, as temple prostitutes.

Map of Abram's Journey[4]

As can be seen by the above map, it was a long trek, and once they arrived at Haran, they lived there till Terah died at 205 years of age.

CHAPTER STRUCTURE

- God's call of Abram to the land of Canaan (v. 1–3).
- Abram's obedience to this call (v. 4, 5).
- His welcome to the land of Canaan (v. 6–9).
- His journey to Egypt, Abram's flight and fault (v. 10–13).
- Sarai's danger and deliverance (v. 14–20).

GOD'S CALL OF ABRAM TO THE LAND OF CANAAN
Genesis 12:1–3

1. Now the LORD had said unto Abram, Get thee out of thy country, and from thy

---

4   . http://www.biblestudy.org/maps/journey-of-abraham-to-promised-land-and-egypt.html.

kindred, and from thy father's house, unto a land that I will shew thee:

2. *And I will make of thee a great nation, and I will bless thee, and make thy name great; and thou shalt be a blessing:*

3. *And I will bless them that bless thee, and curse him that curseth thee: and in thee shall all families of the earth be blessed.*

CALL TO ABRAM
Genesis 12:1

Following the death of his father, Abram once again heard the voice of God telling him to leave the place he now resides. He was originally told this when he lived in Ur, and he came out with his father, wife, nephew, and all they possessed. He is now told by Almighty God to resume the trek.

Genesis 11:31

And Terah took Abram his son, and Lot the son of Haran his son's son, and Sarai his daughter in law, his son Abram's wife; and they went forth with them from Ur of the Chaldees, to go into the land of Canaan; and they came unto Haran, and dwelt there.

Genesis 15:7

And he said unto him, I am the LORD that brought thee out of Ur of the Chaldees, to give thee this land to inherit it.

This time Abram and all that are with him depart from Haran (Charran), and we can make the assumption they do not know where they are going, verse 1, *unto a land that I will shew thee.* We find the following confirmation of the assertion Abram left Haran:

Acts 7:2

And he said, Men, brethren, and fathers, hearken; The God of glory appeared unto our father Abraham, when he was in Mesopotamia, before he dwelt in Charran,

Calvin asserts that this is just a continuation of the last two verses of Genesis 11, and the reader is to understand that due to the age of Terah, they traveled as far as Haran. The party of traveler then remained in Haran five years, which time Terah died. The inference is that Terah, knowing his son, commanded to depart from Ur; Terah did not wish to die in the accursed city. Instead, to associate himself with the one whom God is about to deliver. Upon the death of Terah, Abram and his family continue on their way.[5]

There is no reason that we should not agree with Stephen saying in Act 7:2 and Genesis 12:1 are both a call of God in Ur and in Haran. The call at Haran was a renewed and reaffirming call to Abram, as his concern for his father were gone.[6]

Verse 12:1 tells the reader Abram is required to make a threefold sacrifice: (1) Get *thee out of thy country;* (2) *from thy kindred;* (3) *from thy father's house.* How God will show him the land he is to go.

GOD'S PROMISE TO ABRAM
Genesis 12:2–3

From the reading of these verses, it would appear that God is making a threefold promise, as to compliment the threefold sacrifice. Those promises are (1) going to show you a land and give you the land; (2) I will make a great nation of you, bless you, and make you famous; (3) From you all the people of the earth will be blessed.

On the other hand, the Talmudic teaching is God made a sevenfold promise to Abram:[6]

(1) Abram would be the father of a great nation. Abram was a man of great faith for he was seventy-five years of age when God made this promise and Abram had no heirs. Paul in writing to the Galatians stated:

Galatians 3:6–9

    6.   Even as Abraham believed God, and it was accounted to him for righteousness.

---

5   . Calvin's Commentaries, volume 1, page 342.
6   . The Broadman Bible Commentary, volume 1, page 155.

7.   Know ye therefore that they which are of faith, the same are the children of Abraham.

8.   And the scripture, foreseeing that God would justify the heathen through faith, preached before the gospel unto Abraham, saying, In thee shall all nations be blessed.

9.   So then they which be of faith are blessed with faithful Abraham.

(2) God would bless him in his own lifetime. This means God would keep Abram from harm, i.e., protect him, and God's favor is bestowed on Abram.

(3) God will make Abram a world figure, *make thy name great,* this God most certainly did. He is referred to as father Abraham by Jews, Christians, and Muslims.

(4) Abram would be a blessing to others. Yes, through the Lord Christ Jesus, he has been a blessing to the whole world. In addition, the entire Word of God has come to us through Abraham.[7]

(5) God's blessing would be shared by those who received Abram, for they would thus declare their openness to God.

(6) Those who cursed (degraded, despised) Abram would in that act reveal their own insensitiveness to God at work in him and invite God's wrath upon themselves.

(7) His beneficial influence would be universal.

All of the promises God made to Abraham are fulfilled save one, the first "I am going to show you a land, and I am going to give it to you." The Jews do occupy the land called Israel, which is not all the land God promised. Why, you may ask? Because of their disobedience, they have rejected Christ Jesus as Messiah. But the day is coming when not only the Jews will accept Christ Jesus as Messiah, but the entire world:

Isaiah 45:22–23

22.   Look unto me, and be ye saved, all the ends of the earth: for I am God, and there is none else.

23.   I have sworn by myself, the word is gone out of my mouth in righteousness, and shall not return, That unto me every knee shall bow, every tongue shall swear.

Romans 14:11

---

7   . *Thru the Bible,* page 57.

For it is written, As I live, saith the Lord, every knee shall bow to me, and every tongue shall confess to God.

Philippians 2:10–12

10. Wherefore God also hath highly exalted him, and given him a name which is above every name:
11. That at the name of Jesus every knee should bow, of things in heaven, and things in earth, and things under the earth;
12. And that every tongue should confess that Jesus Christ is Lord, to the glory of God the Father.

ABRAM'S OBEDIENCE TO THIS CALL
Genesis 12:4–5

4. *So Abram departed, as the LORD had spoken unto him; and Lot went with him: and Abram was seventy and five years old when he departed out of Haran.*
5. *And Abram took Sarai his wife, and Lot his brother's son, and all their substance that they had gathered, and the souls that they had gotten in Haran; and they went forth to go into the land of Canaan; and into the land of Canaan they came.*

Abram once again at the direction of the Almighty God sets out for the land which our Creator would show him. He departed Haran not out of fear, but of faith. Most people at the age of seventy-five would just be too comfortable to pull up stacks and leave their friends and family. Abram exemplifies the faith of the believer, not knowing what lies ahead; however, being justified by his faith and having peace with God. The word of God tells that the fruit of the spirit are:

Galatians 5:22–23

22. But the fruit of the Spirit is love, joy, peace, longsuffering, gentleness, goodness, faith,
23. Meekness, temperance: against such there is no law.

Matthew Henry wrote, "What we undertake, in obedience to God's command, and in humble attendance on his providence, will certainly succeed, and end with comfort at last."

Lots accompanying Abram appears to be on his own initiative. I can understand his wanting to be with his uncle, as his father and grandfather have gone on to their reward and he had come this far with his uncle out of Ur. Howsoever, it will become necessary for them to part company.

In verse 5, the phrase "souls that they had gotten in Haran" does not refer to slaves as that would have been referenced as maidservants and menservants. It is more like they are followers of Abram, a religious community if you will form in Haran, and how wanted to continue with Abram.[8] And they journey into the land of Canaan.

HIS WELCOME TO THE LAND OF CANAAN
Genesis 12:6–9

6. *And Abram passed through the land unto the place of Sichem, unto the plain of Moreh. And the Canaanite was then in the land.*
7. *And the LORD appeared unto Abram, and said, Unto thy seed will I give this land: and there builded he an altar unto the LORD, who appeared unto him.*
8. *And he removed from thence unto a mountain on the east of Bethel, and pitched his tent, having Bethel on the west, and Hai on the east: and there he builded an altar unto the LORD, and called upon the name of the LORD.*
9. *And Abram journeyed, going on still toward the south.*

Sichem also spelled Shechem {SHEK uhm} means shoulder and was a fortified city in central Canaan and the first capital of the northern kingdom of Israel. The name is most likely derived from the fact that it was situated on the slope or shoulder of Mount Ebal. This was an important ancient city being situated on the convergences of major trade routes.[9] See Map of Abram's Journey, page 12.

---

8   . The Broadman Bible Commentary, volume 1, page 156.
9   . Nelson's New Illustrated Bible Dictionary, page 1159.

Moreh [MOH reh] means diviner and is the site of oak tree near Shechem. This is the site where Abram build an alter to the Lord.[10] The oak of Moreh was in probability a Canaanite sanctuary. The place at Shechem may indicate this for the term is often applied to sacred spots.[11]

Bethel [BETH uhl] means house of God and is the city on the west side of Abram's tent. The city is located 19 kilometers (12 miles) north of Jerusalem. The region around Bethel is still suitable for grazing by livestock.[12]

Hai [HAY eye] also Ai [A eye] means the ruin and is located east of Bethel.[13]

Abram entered the land of the Canaanites, this most have been a shock to them for they had left the city of Ur five to six years prior, and Ur was an advanced civilization compared to Canaan. The Canaanites are in the heritages of Ham; thus, they are a barbarous and wick lot. So why would Abram and Sarai want to come to this land? Because of their faith in the promise of God and out of obedience to His command.

Having reached Sichem, the Lord God appears to Abram, this is the second time: first in Ur and now. God did not appear to Abram in Haran; He only spoke to him, but now He blesses him. When we are in obedience to God, He will and does pour out His blessings on us. God in the appearing proclaims to his descendants he will give the land of Canaan to them, thus fulfilling the first of the promises. However, today the promise of the land is only partially fulfilled for the land promised covers all the land between the Euphrates and the Nile in Egypt:

Genesis 15:18

> In the same day the LORD made a covenant with Abram, saying, Unto thy
> seed have I given this land, from the river of Egypt unto the great river, the
> river Euphrates:

---

10 . Nelson's New Illustrated Bible Dictionary, page 858.
11 . The Broadman Bible Commentary, volume 1, page 158.
12 . Nelson's New Illustrated Bible Dictionary, page 180.
13 . Nelson's New Illustrated Bible Dictionary, page 36.

This area is approximately 300,000 square miles and encompasses the countries of Jordan, Syria, Lebanon, Iraq, half of Egypt and Saudi Arabia, and Turkey. This may not seem possible given today's situation, but it will in God's timing.

Following God's appearing, Abram built an altar, and he worshipped the Lord our God. Because verse 7 states Abram built an altar, it is inferred that he sacrificed animals for burnt offering as depicted by Noah:

Genesis 8:20
>   And Noah builded an altar unto the LORD; and took of every clean beast, and of every clean fowl, and offered burnt offerings on the altar.

Imagine standing in the very presence of our Lord, what joy Abram must have felt to be able to converse with God. He erected the altar in the presence of the heathen Canaanite; in the process, teaching the Canaanites the proper way in which to worship our God.

Abram then established a home, he "pitched his tent" and church "there built an altar." The scripture does not say how long he remained in the area of Bethel before continuing his trek southward.

HIS JOURNEY TO EGYPT, ABRAM'S FLIGHT AND FAULT
Genesis 12:10–13

>   10. *And there was a famine in the land: and Abram went down into Egypt to sojourn there; for the famine was grievous in the land.*
>   11. *And it came to pass, when he was come near to enter into Egypt, that he said unto Sarai his wife, Behold now, I know that thou art a fair woman to look upon:*
>   12. *Therefore it shall come to pass, when the Egyptians shall see thee, that they shall say, This is his wife: and they will kill me, but they will save thee alive.*
>   13. *Say, I pray thee, thou art my sister: that it may be well with me for thy sake; and my soul shall live because of thee.*

Because of the famine, Abram and his entourage headed for Egypt to escape the famine. In these passages, we see that his faith was tempted and he failed. Had he trusted in God's promise to make a great nation of him, there would be no need for the deception. This is one of the remarkable traits of the Bible; it exposes the sins of its heroes. This should serve as example to the Christian that salvation does not change all of our sinful practices; only through the Holy Spirit working in the born again believer is it even possible to overcome these sinful traits. While it is true that she was his half-sister, obviously, his intention was to save his skin and to deceive others by not revealing they are married.[14]

SARAI'S DANGER AND DELIVERANCE
Genesis 12:14–20

14. *And it came to pass, that, when Abram was come into Egypt, the Egyptians beheld the woman that she was very fair.*

15. *The princes also of Pharaoh saw her, and commended her before Pharaoh: and the woman was taken into Pharaoh's house.*

16. *And he entreated Abram well for her sake: and he had sheep, and oxen, and he asses, and menservants, and maidservants, and she asses, and camels.*

17. *And the LORD plagued Pharaoh and his house with great plagues because of Sarai Abram's wife.*

18. *And Pharaoh called Abram and said, What is this that thou hast done unto me? why didst thou not tell me that she was thy wife?*

19. *Why saidst thou, She is my sister? so I might have taken her to me to wife: now therefore behold thy wife, take her, and go thy way.*

20. *And Pharaoh commanded his men concerning him: and they sent him away, and his wife, and all that he had.*

On the face of it, this whole episode seems ridiculous; if Abram was seventy-fice when they left Haran and Sarai is ten years his junior, that makes her long past child bearing, but sexual pleasure per Genesis 18:12:

Therefore Sarah laughed within herself, saying, After I am waxed old shall I have pleasure, my lord being old also?

---

14   . The Parallel Bible Commentary, page 44–45.

There's no denying the attractiveness of many sixty-five-year-old women today; therefore, there had to be the same in ancient times. After all, they are closer to the creation time frame. Pharaoh would not hesitate to add a striking older woman to his harem to give variety. The young ones would be easier to secure than such a prize.

Some theologies say it was the custom of ancient societies to raise the wife's status to elevate her to sister. Later generations did not know what a noble deed it was and misunderstood it as an act of duplicity. This in an attempt to defend Abram, but this only creates questions that have no answers. While others assert that Abram "with shameful baseness abandon his wife to the lust of a heathen potentate, derives material advantage from this obscene business."[15]

The debate can continue, but the truth is this: God stepped in and protected the horror of Sarai by bring plagues on Pharaoh and his house. Thereby, causing Pharaoh to know he was not to take her to wife and deporting all of them back to Canaan. Interestingly he permitted Abram to keep all the wealth he had given Abram, and Abram must have regret over Hagar and the problems she wrought.

This story also shows the sovereignty of God. His plans will not be derailed, even by the one that is to carry it out. He will preserve and protect his purpose for the ages. Also it should bring assurance to the born again believer, for God will, via the Holy Spirit, keep the saved from wandering off the path of righteousness.

---

15   . The Broadman Bible Commentary, volume 1, page 157.

ABRAM RETURNS OUT OF EGYPT WITH GREAT RICHES

Genesis 13

Abram Returns Out of Egypt[16]

CHAPTER OVERVIEW

This chapter gives an account of the return of Abram from Egypt to the land of Canaan and to the same place he had been before. Strife between the herdsmen of Abram and Lot led to the proposal of Abram to separate; Abram continued in Canaan, and Lot chose the plain of Jordan and dwelt near Sodom, a place infamous for wickedness. The Lord then renewed to Abram the grant of the land of Canaan to him and to his seed. Then Abram goes to the plain of Mamre in Hebron, and there set up an altar for the worship of God.

---

16   . www.gci.org/files/etwog19a.jpg.

CHAPTER STRUCTURE

- Abram returns out of Egypt with great riches. (1–4)
- Strife between the herdsmen of Abram and Lot. (5–7)
- Abram gives Lot his choice of the country. (8–9)
- Lot chooses to dwell at Sodom. (10–13)
- God renews his promise to Abram, who removes to Hebron. (14–18)

ABRAM RETURNS OUT OF EGYPT
Genesis 13:1–4

1. *And Abram went up out of Egypt, he, and his wife, and all that he had, and Lot with him, into the south.*
2. *And Abram was very rich in cattle, in silver, and in gold.*
3. *And he went on his journeys from the south even to Bethel, unto the place where his tent had been at the beginning, between Bethel and Hai;*
4. *Unto the place of the altar, which he had make there at the first: and there Abram called on the name of the LORD.*

In chapter 12, Pharaoh provided wealth for Abram because of Sarai.

Genesis 12:16–7
16. The princes also of Pharaoh saw her, and commended her before Pharaoh: and the woman was taken into Pharaoh's house.
17. And he entreated Abram well for her sake: and he had sheep, and oxen, and he asses, and menservants, and maidservants, and she asses, and camels.

And when Pharaoh discovered that Sarai was actually Abram's wife, he kicked them out of Egypt. However, Abram was permitted to keep all that Pharaoh had given them. Their sojourn into Egypt was the means by which God provided wealth for Abram and his seed with no sorrow attached with it.

Proverbs 10:22
The blessing of the LORD, it maketh rich, and he addeth no sorrow with it.

Abram was very rich: he was very heavy, the Hebrew word signifies; for riches are a burden; and they that will be rich, do but load themselves with thick clay.

Habakkuk 2:6

> Shall not all these take up a parable against him, and a taunting proverb against him, and say, Woe to him that increaseth that which is not his! how long? and to him that ladeth himself with thick clay!

There is a burden of care in getting riches, fear in keeping them, temptation in using them, guilt in abusing them, sorrow in losing them, and a burden of account at last to be given up about them. Yet God in his providence sometimes makes good men rich men, and thus God's blessing made Abram rich without sorrow. Though it is hard for a rich man to get to heaven, in some cases, it may be.

Mark 10:23,24

> 23. And Jesus looked round about, and saith unto his disciples, How hardly shall they that have riches enter into the kingdom of God!
> 24. And the disciples were astonished at his words. But Jesus answereth again, and saith unto them, Children, how hard is it for them that trust in riches to enter into the kingdom of God!

Nay, outward prosperity, if well managed, is an ornament to piety and an opportunity for doing more good. Abram removed to Beth-el. His altar was gone so that he could not offer sacrifice; but he called on the name of the Lord. You may as soon find a living man without breath as one of God's people without prayer.[17] Undoubtedly Abram returned to renew his vows after his sojourn into Egypt Abram needed to make a new start.

STRIFE BETWEEN THE HERDSMEN OF ABRAM AND LOT
Genesis 13:5–7

> 5. *And Lot also, which went with Abram, had flocks, and herds, and tents.*
> 6. *And the land was not able to bear them, that they might dwell together: for their substance was great, so that they could not dwell together.*

---

17   . Matthew Henry's Concise Commentary.

> 7. *And there was a strife between the herdmen of Abram's cattle and the herdmen of Lot's cattle: and the Canaanite and the Perizzites dwelled then in the land.*

It would appear from these verses that some time period has elapsed in order to have such an increase of cattle (domesticated livestock, sheep, camels, goats, etc.) as to bring about fighting between the herdsmen. The struggle to find enough grass for the animals in the aired land of the Mideast is a challenge. Add to this mix was the Canaanites and Perizzites also trying to pastured their flocks and herds. The scarcity of good pasture led to the headsmen of Abram and Lot fighting over this scarce resource, and I would imagine this struggle caused conflict with the Canaanites and Perizzites, but this is not stated in this passage.

The Perizzites were most likely Amorites and were wicked people. They controlled the good grazing land, which made it extremely difficult for Abram and Lot to find good grazing for their cattle.[18]

In addition to the Canaanite and the Perizzites dwelling in the land, seeing the servants of Abram and Lot fighting among themselves may be perceived as an opportunity to make off with their livestock or the subjugation of Abram's and Lot's servants. Further, the squabbling being observed by these non-believing groups, viewed as a negative testimony of the Almighty God, made conversion to the one true God difficult, if not impossible.

ABRAM GIVES LOT HIS CHOICE OF THE COUNTRY
Genesis 13:8–9

> 8. *And Abram said unto Lot, Let there be no strife, I pray thee, between me and thee, and between my herdmen and thy herdmen; for we be brethren.*
> 9. *Is not the whole land before thee? separate thyself, I pray thee, from me: if thou wilt take the left hand, then I will go to the right; or if thou depart to the right hand, then I will go to the left.*

From these verses, the reader gains insight into the maturity of Abram both secular and as a servant of the Most High God. It is the believer that is will to forgive, or

---

18   . The Parallel Bible Commentary, page 46.

make restitution first, so as to end conflict and have peace. Peter makes the following observation of Lot in:

2 Peter 2:7–8

7. And delivered just Lot, vexed with the filthy conversation of the wicked:
8. (For that righteous man dwelling among them, in seeing and hearing, vexed his righteous soul from day to day with their unlawful deeds;)

In this case, Abram headed off a confrontation with his nephew by giving him the choice of the way they should separate. Abram's appeal goes beyond the mere physical ties of kinship; he demonstrated the way of the believer to seek peace and in all humility.

LOT CHOOSES TO DWELL AT SODOM
Genesis 13:10–13

10. *And Lot lifted up his eyes, and beheld all the plain of Jordan, that it was well watered everywhere, before the LORD destroyed Sodom and Gomorrah, even as the garden of the LORD, like the land of Egypt, as thou comest unto Zoar.*
11. *Then Lot chose him all the plain of Jordan; and Lot journeyed east: and they separated themselves the one from the other.*
12. *Abram dwelled in the land of Canaan, and Lot dwelled in the cities of the plain, and pitched his tent toward Sodom.*
13. *But the men of Sodom were wicked and sinners before the LORD exceedingly*

In reading these verses, one is struck by the way Lot responded to his uncle Abram; there was no protest or "No, Uncle, you choose first." Lot looked on the plain of Jordan and the desires of the flesh came to the fore; seeing this was good pasture land being well watered. He chose the Jordan plain without concern for his uncle's needs. His concern was only focused on the needs of self, thereby ensuring his flock and heads would continue to increase. In making this choice, Lot placed himself and household in jeopardy because *the men of Sodom were wicked and sinners* as stated in chapter 19 of Genesis.

The Parting of Abraham and Lot[19]

In making his decision, Lot disregarded the obvious problems: (1) no matter how appealing the situation may be, the first step in the decision process is to seek God's direction; (2) Lot should have let Abram have the choice, as he had obtained his wealth via Abram; (3) Living in proximity to such a wick city exposes not only Lot, but his household to the vileness of Sodom which leads to temptations. If one acts on the temptation, then they are in jeopardy of losing their soul.[20]

Some scholars believe the phrase *even as the garden of the LORD* indicates this is the location of the Garden of Eden, but as stated in Chapter 2 of Genesis Primeval History, Pages 16 - 17 this plain of Jordan is only a part of the Garden of Eden. Of course the information presented in chapter two is purely speculation as the flood and the tectonic shift changed the earth's surface.

Zoar (ZOE ahr), meaning little, is a city located on the east side of the south end of the Dead Sea, also known as Bela. It is one of the five city-states in the area, each with its own king. Many scholars believe the site of Zoar to be es-Safi, at the foot of the

19   . lavistachurchofchrist.org.
20   . *The Broadman Bible Commentary*, volume 1, page 159.

mountains of Moab, about 4.5 miles (7 kilometers) up the River Zered from where it empties into the Dead Sea.[21]

GOD RENEWS HIS PROMISE TO ABRAM
Genesis 13:14–18

14. *And the LORD said unto Abram, after that Lot was separated from him, Lift up now thine eyes, and look from the place where thou art northward, and southward, and eastward, and westward:*

15. *For all the land which thou seest, to thee will I give it, and to thy seed for ever.*

16. *And I will make thy seed as the dust of the earth: so that if a man can number the dust of the earth, then shall thy seed also be numbered.*

17. *Arise, walk through the land in the length of it and in the breadth of it; for I will give it unto thee.*

18. *Then Abram removed his tent, and came and dwelt in the plain of Mamre, which is in Hebron, and built there an altar unto the LORD.*

With the departure of Lot, Abram is finally in compliance with God's instruction to separate from his relatives, and being in obedience, God shows Abram the land He promised.

Genesis 12:1
    Now the LORD had said unto Abram, Get thee out of thy country, and from thy kindred, and from thy father's house, unto a land that I will shew thee

God then tells Abram the land which he is in the midst of is his and his descendants forever. Although this promise was only partially fulfilled four hundred years later by the children of Israel (Jacob), not till 1948 did the land truly pass to Abram's descendants with the passage of United Nations General Assembly Resolution 181 (II) Future Government of Palestine (November 29, 1947). The result was the start of the Arab-Israeli War on May 15, 1948, with the withdrawal of all British troops. Also on this date, the Jewish community in Palestine published a Declaration of Independence which announced the creation of the State of Israel. The current land controlled by Israel is not what God promised; it is far from what God had in mind. On the day

---

21   . *Nelson's New Illustrated Bible Dictionary*, page 1344.

the Lord Christ Jesus returns then Israel will have its full territory as described in the following verses:

Genesis 15:18–21

> 18. In the same day the LORD made a covenant with Abram, saying, Unto thy seed have I given this land, from the river of Egypt unto the great river, the river Euphrates:
> 19. The Kenites, and the Kenizzites, and the Kadmonites,
> 20. And the Hittites, and the Perizzites, and the Rephaims,
> 21. And the Amorites, and the Canaanites, and the Girgashites, and the Jebusites.

Exodus 23:31

> And I will set thy bounds from the Red sea even unto the sea of the Philistines, and from the desert unto the river: for I will deliver the inhabitants of the land into your hand; and thou shalt drive them out before thee.

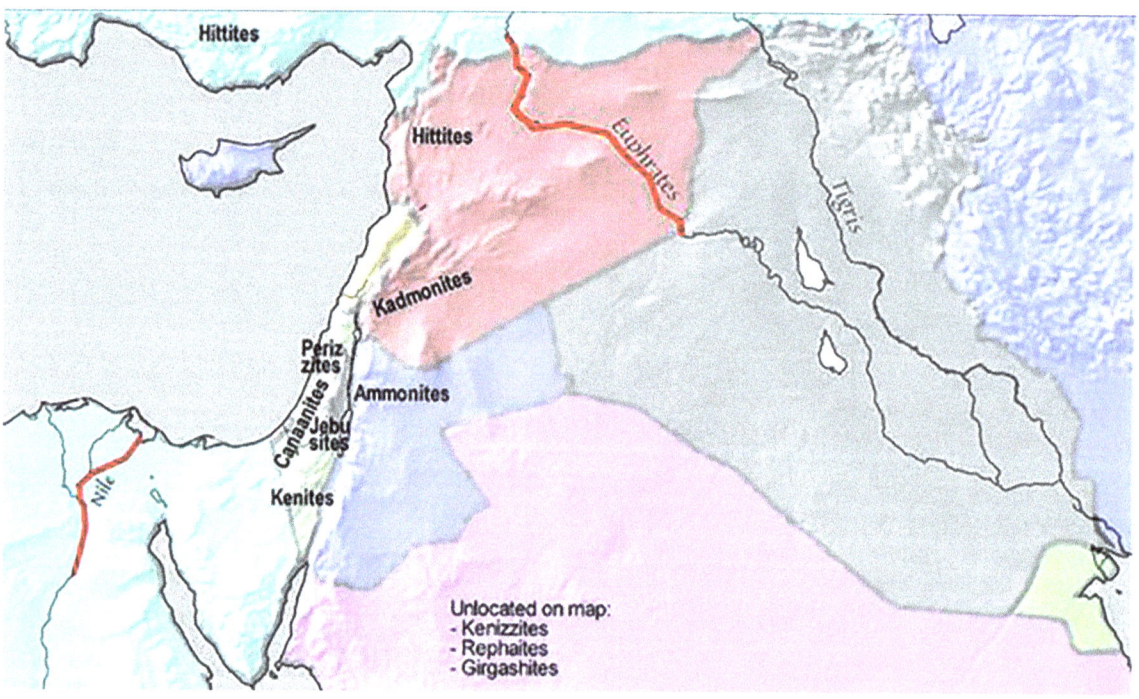

Interpretation of the Promised Land[22]

God tells Abram that his descendants will be so numerous they will be beyond one's ability to count them. Abram is told this by God, yet he has no children, and he does

---

22   . http://en.wikipedia.org/wiki/File:Greater_Israel_map.jpg.

not argue the point. Abram accepted this purely on faith in God's word, which today has been rewarded, for his descendants can be observed around the world.

Following Abram's conversation with the Almighty God, he then packs up and moves to the plain of Mamre; this is in Hebron. This is north of Sodom about the middle of the Dead Sea's western shore. Mamre [MAM reh] means richness and was noted for its terebinth trees or oak (proper name *Pistacia palaestina*).[23] Hebron [HEE bruhn] means communion and is located 19 miles (31 kilometers) southwest of Jerusalem on the road to Beersheba. It is situated at 3040 feet (927 meters) above sea level, which makes it the highest town in Palestine.[24]

J. Vernon McGee states that one of the Dead Sea Scrolls describes this region in first-person account by Abraham of the land. It was a wonderful land in his day. A forest of these large spreading trees which reach a height 20–26 feet with reddish-green leaves and red berries clusters. This is the dwelling place of Abram and a good place of richness and of communion with God. It is also the burial place of Abraham and Sarah, his son Isaac and his wife Rebekah, and his grandson Jacob and his wife Leah.[25]

Abram built an altar to the Lord God. The reader will note that Abram build altars wherever he stop and worship the Lord. It is apparent Abram was well chosen by God for his deep faith, and as a result, God poured out His blessing on him. The reader would be well advised to follow Abram's example.

---

23   . *Nelson's New Illustrated Bible Dictionary*, page 794.
24   . *Nelson's New Illustrated Bible Dictionary*, page 554.
25   . *Thru the Bible*, volume 1, page 62.

THE FIRST RECORD BATTLE OF KINGS

Genesis 14

Battle Illustration[26]

CHAPTER OVERVIEW

This is the chapter of firsts and doesn't fit in with any of the so-called "sources" of the Bible critics; hence their determined attacks on its veracity. However, its historical accuracy has been confirmed by recent archeological discoveries.[27] The chapter begins with the recount of the alignment of kings that made war on The Cities of Jordan

---

26   . http://listverse.files.wordpress.com/2008/07/marathon-battle3.jpg.
27   . *The Pentateuch and Haftorahs*, second edition, page 50; Trustees of the Late Dr. j. h. Hertz, 1960: The Soncino Press Limited, 123 Ditmas Avenue, Brooklyn, New York 11218.

Plain, which is the first recorded account of a war, and had not Abram and Lot been involved, there would be no record of it. Then there is the rescue of Lot by Abram, who was taken captive by the warring kings. There is the first reference to tithes and the acceptance of them by a priest of the Almighty God. Finally there is the distribution of the booty, following the conquering of the warring kings.

CHAPTER STRUCTURE

- The battle of the kings, Lot is taken prisoner. (1–12)
- Abram rescues Lot. (13–16)
- Melchizedek blesses Abram. (17–20)
- Abram restores the spoil. (21–24)

THE BATTLE OF THE KINGS, LOT IS TAKEN PRISONER
Genesis 14:1–12

1. *And it came to pass in the days of Amraphel king of Shinar, Arioch king of Ellasar, Chedorlaomer king of Elam, and Tidal king of nations;*
2. *That these made war with Bera king of Sodom, and with Birsha king of Gomorrah, Shinab king of Admah, and Shemeber king of Zeboiim, and the king of Bela, which is Zoar.*
3. *All these were joined together in the vale of Siddim, which is the salt sea.*
4. *Twelve years they served Chedorlaomer, and in the thirteenth year they rebelled.*
5. *And in the fourteenth year came Chedorlaomer, and the kings that were with him, and smote the Rephaims in Ashteroth Karnaim, and the Zuzims in Ham, and the Emins in Shaveh Kiriathaim,*
6. *And the Horites in their mount Seir, unto Elparan, which is by the wilderness.*
7. *And they returned, and came to Enmishpat, which is Kadesh, and smote all the country of the Amalekites, and also the Amorites, that dwelt in Hazezontamar.*
8. *And there went out the king of Sodom, and the king of Gomorrah, and the king of Admah, and the king of Zeboiim, and the king of Bela (the same is Zoar;) and they joined battle with them in the vale of Siddim;*
9. *With Chedorlaomer the king of Elam, and with Tidal king of nations, and Amraphel king of Shinar, and Arioch king of Ellasar; four kings with five.*

10. *And the vale of Siddim was full of slimepits; and the kings of Sodom and Gomorrah fled, and fell there; and they that remained fled to the mountain.*

11. *And they took all the goods of Sodom and Gomorrah, and all their victuals, and went their way.*

12. *And they took Lot, Abram's brother's son, who dwelt in Sodom, and his goods, and departed.*

THE COMBATANTS
Genesis 14:1–2

The invading combatants are as follows:

- Amraphel [Am rah fell], king of Shinar [SHIGH nahr], this is the city established by Nimrod and later became the city of Babylon
- Arioch [AIR ih ock], king of Ellasar [el LAY sar]
- Chedorlaomer [ked awr LAY oh muhr] means servant of lagamar (god of Elamite), king of Elam
- Tidal [TIE duhl], king of nations also known as Goiim [GOY yim] (nations)[28]

Map of Invaders[29]

As can be seen, this is the combined armies of Mesopotamian King Chedorlaomer, ruler of the Persian empire of Elam to the East and commander of the alliance; King Amraphel, ruler of Shinar from the southern regions of Babylon; King Arioch, ruler of Ellasar, from Assur to the North; King Tidal, leader of the Hittites from the West. The term "king of nation" is defined by the cuneiform texts as king of the "hordes" of northern Kurdish nation—modern-day Turkey.[30]

---

28 . *Nelson's New Illustrated Bible Dictionary*, pages 53, 113, 256, 386, 1250, 514.
29 . http://www.jesuswalk.com/abraham/3_rescue.htm.
30 . *The Pentateuch and Haftorahs*, page 50.

Defending combatants are as follows:

Bera [BEE rah] king of Sodom [SOD um], early tradition held that Sodom was located on the north end of the Dead Sea. However, the geologic condition of the southeastern shore region of the Dead Sea matches the condition of the Sodom of Scripture; Birsha [BURR shah], king of Gomorrah [guh MOR ruh] meaning submersion is closely aligned with its sister Sodom;

Shinab [SHIGH nab] meaning sin is my father king of Admah [AD muh] meaning red earth. Many biblical scholars associate the city with Adam.

Map of Cities of the Plain[30]

Joshua 3:16

> That the waters which came down from above stood and rose up upon an heap very far from the city Adam, that is beside Zaretan: and those that came down toward the sea of the plain, even the salt sea, failed, and were cut off: and the people passed over right against Jericho.

Shemeber [shem EE bur], king of Zeboiim [zeh BOY yim]; many scholars believe this once wicked city is covered by the waters of the southern Dead Sea; and king of Bela, [BEE lah]which is Zoar [ZOE ahr], meaning little and is the city of refuse for Lot when God destroyed the cities of the plain.

As can be seen on the Map of Cities of the Plain, the cities are identified by red.

CONTEXT OF THE CONFRONTATION
Genesis 14:3–7

The Elamite Empire had conquered the Canaanites including the cities of the Jordan plain and were under their control for twelve years. The Elamites made them vassal states and required them to pay tribute to the Elamite Empire. This is just like the gangs making shopkeepers pay protection money. This conquest came about in all probability was to control the trade route which increased revenue to the empire. This seemed to work for thirteen years, for in the thirteenth year, these five vassal states refused to pay the tribute money according to Jewish tradition.

In the fourteenth year, Chedorlaomer mounted a campaign against the rebelling vassal state of the plain. The reader should note he took a circuitous route implying he needed to reassert his control and authority over the trade route and the copper mines in the area.[31]

The peoples referenced in verses 5–8, Rephaims [REF ih yuhm], Zuzims [ZOU zim], Emins [EE mim], and Horites [HOAR ites], are the aboriginal inhabitants of the regions afterward occupied by Edom, Moab, and Ammon, see chapter 2 of Deuteronomy.

BATTLE OF SIDDIM
Genesis 14:8–12

It was not until Chedorlaomer entered into the valley of Siddim did the Cities of Plain rise up to meet the invading army. Now they engaged in battle, and the armies of the plain did not overcome their adversary. Retreating into the valley of Siddim which contained slime pits or tar pits, this might have been a strategy to entrap the invading armies within the pits due to their lack of knowledge of the topography. The strategy failed, and they fled to the mountains.

---

31   . *The Broadman Bible Commentary*, volume 1, page 161.

ABRAM RESCUES LOT
Genesis 14:13–16

13. *And there came one that had escaped, and told Abram the Hebrew; for he dwelt in the plain of Mamre the Amorite, brother of Eshcol, and brother of Aner: and these were confederate with Abram.*
14. *And when Abram heard that his brother was taken captive, he armed his trained servants, born in his own house, three hundred and eighteen, and pursued them unto Dan.*
15. *And he divided himself against them, he and his servants, by night, and smote them, and pursued them unto Hobah, which is on the left hand of Damascus.*
16. *And he brought back all the goods, and also brought again his brother Lot, and his goods, and the women also, and the people.*

This is the first occurrence of the word *Hebrew* in the Bible. The Rabbis are divided on the origin of the name Hebrew. There are two possibilities: (1) it is connected with Eber and signifies "a descendant of Eber," see chapter 11 which shows Abram in the lineage of Eber; (2) it means "one from the other side" as found in:

Joshua 24:3

> And I took your father Abraham from the other side of the flood, and led him throughout all the land of Canaan, and multiplied his seed, and gave him Isaac.

The phrase "other side of the flood" in Joshua means the other side of the Euphrates River. Some scholars claim that the name is identical to "Habiri," nomadic people that made war on the Canaanites.[32]

Now hearing that his nephew was taken captive, Abram immediately assembles is his forces. This should dispel his cowardly behavior in Egypt as one of forethought.

Map of Invader & Abram Route[33]

---

32   . *The Pentateuch and Haftorahs*, page 51.
33   . http://www.jesuswalk.com/abraham/3_rescue.htm.

In verse 14, the reader should take note: "born in his own house" is a reference to slaves that were born and reared in the Patriarch's home. If Abram has 318 men trained in the art of war or defense, how many more are there that are workers? Just from the number of trainer warriors, there had to be at least 636 men and women as couples. Those born of his house would feel a greater sense of loyalty.

When examining verse 15, the reader is not told how Abram divided his forces; some scholars think into two groups; one making a frontal assault and the other from the rear once the enemy turned to face their attackers. On the other hand, the rabbinical scholars think Abram divided his forces into four and attacked from all side under the cover of darkness, utilizing a strategy similar or the same strategy implied by Gideon:

Judges 7:16
> And he divided the three hundred men into three companies, and he put
> a trumpet in every man's hand, with empty pitchers, and lamps within the
> pitchers.

Verse 16 makes it clear the booty the Mesopotamian stole has now been reclaimed, and that includes Abram's nephew Lot, as well as the other citizens of the cities of the plain. Broadman Bible Commentary makes the following observation about Abram:[34]

1. He acted quickly. The Hebrew for led forth means to empty as one pulls his sword from its sheath, Exodus 15:9. Had he delayed, they would have missed the opportunity to overtake their adversary.
2. He acted decisively. Taking the best trained and loyal men, dividing them into battle groups for efficient and effective order of battle. He attacked by night as they slept or after they celebrated their victory, and overpower the foe.
3. He followed through to ensure victory and the enemy would not regroup and counterattack.

---

34   . *Broadman Bible Commentary*, volume 1, pages 161–162.

MELCHIZEDEK BLESSES ABRAM
Genesis 14:17–20

17. *And the king of Sodom went out to meet him after his return from the slaughter of Chedorlaomer, and of the kings that were with him, at the valley of Shaveh, which is the king's dale.*
18. *And Melchizedek king of Salem brought forth bread and wine: and he was the priest of the most high God.*
19. *And he blessed him, and said, Blessed be Abram of the most high God, possessor of heaven and earth:*
20. *And blessed be the most high God, which hath delivered thine enemies into thy hand. And he gave him tithes of all.*

Abraham meets with Melchizedek[35]

Melchizedek king of Salem, who is this? Let scripture interpret scripture:

Hebrews 7:

1. For this Melchizedek, king of Salem, priest of the most high God, who met Abraham returning from the slaughter of the kings, and blessed him;

2. To whom also Abraham gave a tenth part of all; first being by interpretation King of righteousness, and after that also King of Salem, which is, King of peace;

3. Without father, without mother, without descent, having neither beginning of days, nor end of life; but made like unto the Son of God; abideth a priest continually.

4. Now consider how great this man was, unto whom even the patriarch Abraham gave the tenth of the spoils.

So who is this Melchizedek? Theologians have various thought. Some think he was an angel; some say he is the incarnation of Enoch; while St. Jerome and Martin Luther thought of him as Shem which is possible as Shem was 602 years of age when he died. Abram was between the ages of 75 and 90 at this time while Shem was less than 500 years of age.

There are others that think Melchizedek was a *theophany* (a pre-incarnate appearance of Christ Jesus). By applying the literal meaning of Hebrews 7:2 King of righteousness, and after that also King of Salem, which is King of peace, and Hebrews 7:3: Without father, without mother, without descent, having neither beginning of days, nor end of life.

But most of the scholars think of Melchizedek as just a man. Hebrews 7:4: Now consider how great this man was. The use of the words *this man was* signifies he is just that a man.

Which opinion the reader chooses to accept, Melchizedek is representative of a type of Christ Jesus. Verse 18 reveals Melchizedek as King and Priest, king of Salem or king of Peace which later was renamed Jerusalem, and priest of the Most High God continually.

Psalm 110:4

The LORD hath sworn, and will not repent, Thou art a priest for ever after the order of Melchizedek.

Melchizedek provided Abram with bread and wine which is representative of the Lord Table and once again acting as a type of Christ Jesus:

Luke 22:19–20
> 19. And he took bread, and gave thanks, and brake it, and gave unto them, saying, This is my body which is given for you: this do in remembrance of me.
> 20. Likewise also the cup after supper, saying, This cup is the new testament in my blood, which is shed for you.

Following the refreshments of bread and wine, Melchizedek then blessed Abram in the name of the Most High God Almighty, and blessed The Almighty for the victory over the Mesopotamians and the return of those taken captive and booty.

After the Melchizedek's blessing, Abram gave him tithes; this is the first use of the word *tithes*, meaning one tenth. The act of tithing reflects Abram's pity and valor. For this is but a token of his gratitude and honor of a divine intervention. Although he gave the tithe to Melchizedek the priest, he was the mediator between God and man, thus Abram honors a divine ordinance.[36]

Proverbs 3:9
> Honour the LORD with thy substance, and with the first fruits of all thine increase:

Malachi 3
> 1. Ye are cursed with a curse: for ye have robbed me, even this whole nation.
> 2. Bring ye all the tithes into the storehouse, that there may be meat in mine house, and prove me now herewith, saith the LORD of hosts, if I will not open you the windows of heaven, and pour you out a blessing, that there shall not be room enough to receive it.

---

36   . Jamieson Faussett Brow Bible Commentary: http://www.ewordtoday.com/comments/genesis/jfb/genesis14.htm.

ABRAM RESTORES THE SPOIL
Genesis 14:21–24

21. And the king of Sodom said unto Abram, Give me the persons, and take the goods to thyself.

22. And Abram said to the king of Sodom, I have lift up mine hand unto the LORD, the most high God, the possessor of heaven and earth,

23. That I will not take from a thread even to a shoelatchet, and that I will not take any thing that is thine, lest thou shouldest say, I have made Abram rich:

24. Save only that which the young men have eaten, and the portion of the men which went with me, Aner, Eshcol, and Mamre; let them take their portion.

In the tradition of the Mideast Bedouins, the booty belongs to the one that conquers; thus, the king of Sodom requested he release to him the people, i.e., the citizen of Sodom. The king was showing both gratitude and humility, because this was a request, not a command.

Abram responded by stating he had lifted up his hand to the most high God, the possessor of heaven and earth, the same as Melchizedek. In other words, he had sworn an oath before God, which is a most solemn act. Abram was relying on God to provide and not man or even himself. Further, he knew the wicked hearts and minds of the people of Sodom, and he did not want this king to come back on him later making a claim for some trumped-up charge out of jealousy: *I have made Abram rich*. The results of anger over that which would be Abram's rightful claim.

Abram again showed what an honorable man he was, by asking the king to allow that his allies take their portion.

GOD'S BLOOD COVENANT WITH ABRAM

Genesis 15

God shows Abraham the stars to illustrate his innumerable descendants[37]

37 . http://www.jesuswalk.com/abraham/images/abraham_stars721x597.jpg. *God shows Abraham the stars to illustrate his innumerable descendants.* By German painter Julius Schnorr von Carolsfeld (1794–1872), engraving, from "Bibel in Bildern" (1851–60).

CHAPTER OVERVIEW

This is the chapter of promise. God reaffirms his promise to Abram and that he will have an heir for the land which God has given Abram. God further states that his prodigy shall suffer great affliction, but will come out of it with great substance. The Promised Land would then pass to his descendants. Most theologians think this is one of the most important chapters in the Bible, as it is through the lineage of Abraham that our Lord Christ Jesus comes fore.

CHAPTER STRUCTURE

- The Divine promise, Abraham is justified by faith. (1–6)
- God promises Canaan to Abraham for an inheritance. (7–11)
- The promise confirmed in a vision. (12–16)
- The promise confirmed by a sign. (17–21)

THE DIVINE PROMISE, ABRAHAM IS JUSTIFIED BY FAITH
Genesis 15:1–6

1. *After these things the word of the LORD came unto Abram in a vision, saying, Fear not, Abram: I am thy shield, and thy exceeding great reward.*
2. *And Abram said, LORD God, what wilt thou give me, seeing I go childless, and the steward of my house is this Eliezer of Damascus?*
3. *And Abram said, Behold, to me thou hast given no seed: and, lo, one born in my house is mine heir.*
4. *And, behold, the word of the LORD came unto him, saying, This shall not be thine heir; but he that shall come forth out of thine own bowels shall be thine heir.*
5. *And he brought him forth abroad, and said, Look now toward heaven, and tell the stars, if thou be able to number them: and he said unto him, So shall thy seed be.*
6. *And he believed in the LORD; and he counted it to him for righteousness*

GOD'S REVELATION
Genesis 15:1

Following Abram's restoration of the property that was stolen to Sodom, the Lord God appears Abram in a vision. This is just one of the ways God communicates with those He has chosen. In the book of Numbers, we find these passages:

Numbers 12

7.   And he said, Hear now my words: If there be a prophet among you, I the LORD will make myself known unto him in a vision, and will speak unto him in a dream.

8.   My servant Moses is not so, who is faithful in all mine house.

9.   With him will I speak mouth to mouth, even apparently, and not in dark speeches; and the similitude of the LORD shall he behold: wherefore then were ye not afraid to speak against my servant Moses?

As can be seen, God makes Himself known via visions, dreams, and with Moses He spoke face to face or *mouth to mouth*. Also in Joel which is repeated in Acts:

Joel 2:28

And it shall come to pass afterward, that I will pour out my spirit upon all flesh; and your sons and your daughters shall prophesy, your old men shall dream dreams, your young men shall see visions.

Acts 2:17

And it shall come to pass in the last days, saith God, I will pour out of my Spirit upon all flesh: and your sons and your daughters shall prophesy, and your young men shall see visions, and your old men shall dream dreams.

The Lord then tells Abram not to be fearful, which implies he was afraid. After his defeat of the Mesopotamian kings, he surely was fearful of them returning and taking their revenge on him, i.e., kill him. Therefore God is reassuring Abram that he is not to fear, because God will protect him: *I am thy shield.* On the other hand, it could be he was very much afraid of being in the presence of Almighty God. Therefore, God is reassuring him he has nothing to fear. However, the phrase *I am thy shield* would indicate the previous; God will be his protector.

The last phrase of this opening verse, *thy exceeding great reward*, is a wonderful statement; God is Abram's reward. There are two possibilities for this statement: (1) because Abram began seeking the one true God and not the false god that his father made; (2) Abram's refusal to take any of the spoils that he captured after defeating the kings of Mesopotamia. As Peter wrote:

1 Peter 5:2
> Feed the flock of God which is among you, taking the oversight thereof, not by constraint, but willingly; not for filthy lucre, but of a ready mind;

From the scriptures, it is evident that Abram/Abraham did feed the believer that God has given him and to witness to the Canaanites. As a result of Abram's faithfulness, God has filled his treasury.

ABRAM QUESTIONS GOD OF HIS HEIR
Genesis 15:2–3

Abram now turns his attention to who will be his heir. He asks God, "What will you give me?" He does not want more wealth. What he wants is an heir, but he has no children, and in despair, Abram states that the steward of his house, Eliezed [el ih EE zur] of Damascus, will inherit. This may appear strange to modern society, but this was a common practice of the culture of the Mideast in those days.

The meaning of the name Eliezed is "My God is helper."[38] The steward was a most trusted servant, slave, which would continue the family line as directed. One could say the steward was the chief executive officer, chief financial officer, director of production, and chief of police all rounded into one person.

If we think about this, Abram's statements make sense for the human mind's point of view. Abram is past seventy-five years of age and Sarai is past sixty-five years of age and never had a child. Scripture does not state their ages at this point. Can you not hear the frustration in his question? There is another point of interest; Abram makes no mention of his nephew, Lot. Could this be because of his foolish choice to remain in the wicked city of Sodom?

---

38   . *Nelson's New Illustrated Bible Dictionary*, page 392.

GOD'S REPLY TO ABRAM'S UNCERTAINTY
Genesis 15:4–5

The Almighty God does not get angry with Abram questioning Him about the promised son. God simply and authoritatively states that Eliezed will not be Abram's heir. He then continues to repeat the promise son of his loins, a reaffirmation of

Genesis 12:7

> And the LORD appeared unto Abram, and said, Unto thy seed will I give this land: and there builded he an altar unto the LORD, who appeared unto him.

God then took Abram by the hand and brought him forth into the night.[39] God has Abram look up at the night sky and count the stars, which he could not. Just in the range of sight, there was approximately fifty thousand plus stars that we can see and that with all the light pollution. J. Vernon McGee in *Thru the Bible*[40] states Abram actually has two seeds: his physical seed, Israel, and his spiritual seed, the church. His proof is found in the book of Galatians and chapter 3:

28. There is neither Jew nor Greek, there is neither bond nor free, there is neither male nor female: for ye are all one in Christ Jesus.
29. And if ye be Christ's, then are ye Abraham's seed, and heirs according to the promise.

This is a wonderful assurance for the born-again believer. We shall rule with our Lord Christ Jesus.

ABRAM IS JUSTIFIED BY FAITH
Genesis 15:6

Many scholars and theologians consider this passage the key verse of the entire Old Testament; it is important witness to the doctrine of justification by faith. Abram's act of faith was accounted to him as righteousness. There is no other way to salvation

---

39 . *Thru The Bible*, volume 1, page 66.
40 . *Thru The Bible*, volume 1, page 66.

than through the grace of God brought by faith in what Christ Jesus did on the cross, and not by good deeds or works.

> It is not on account of any virtue or goodness in faith, but as it unites us to Christ Jesus, and involves the acceptance of Him as our righteousness. Thus it is we are justified by faith alone, without any manner of virtue or goodness of our own.[41]

Per the Westminster Catechism, "An act of God's free grace, wherein He pardoneth all our sins, and accepteth us as righteous in His sight, only for the righteousness of Christ imputed to us, and received by faith alone."[42]

Points on the Doctrine of Justification[43]

1. It is a single act when one comes to faith in Christ Jesus, unlike sanctification that is a continual and progressive work.
2. The sinner is worthy of the condemnation of God, but for the grace of God justifying the sinner.
3. Nature of the act
    A. It does not produce a change in character, which is the result of regeneration, i.e., being born again, and sanctification.
    B. It is not a mere executive act, as when a king or president pardons a criminal.
    C. It is a declarative act of God as judge pronouncing the sinner as just and righteous and entitled to the rewards, i.e., eternal life.
4. The meritorious ground of justification is the righteousness of Christ Jesus. His redeeming act on the cross; paid in full the penalty of the law in our stead and on our behalf.
5. The righteousness of Christ alone is the impetuous for our justification as born-again believers. Therefore, we can plead the blood of Christ Jesus as we stand before the bar of God's court.

---

41 . Charles Hodge (2008), *Systematic Theology*, volume 3, page 116; Hendrickson Publishers, Inc.; PO Box 3473; Peabody, Massachusetts 01961-3473.
42 . Hodge, volume 3, page114.
43 . Hodge, volume 3, pages 117–118.

6. Faith is the condition of justification. God does not impute the righteousness of Christ Jesus, until and unless, the sinner through grace, receives and rest on Christ alone for his salvation.

Paul used this verse for his argument with Jerusalem Church Father over circumcision of the converts in Greece. Abram's faith was accounted to him as righteousness before he was circumcised and hundreds of years before the law was given to his descendants.

Romans 3:22–30

22. For all have sinned, and come short of the glory of God;
23. Being justified freely by his grace through the redemption that is in Christ Jesus:
24. Whom God hath set forth to be a propitiation through faith in his blood, to declare his righteousness for the remission of sins that are past, through the forbearance of God;
25. To declare, I say, at this time his righteousness: that he might be just, and the justifier of him which believeth in Jesus.
26. Where is boasting then? It is excluded. By what law? of works? Nay: but by the law of faith.
27. Therefore we conclude that a man is justified by faith without the deeds of the law.
28. Is he the God of the Jews only? is he not also of the Gentiles? Yes, of the Gentiles also:
29. Seeing it is one God, which shall justify the circumcision by faith, and uncircumcision through faith.
30. Do we then make void the law through faith? God forbid: yea, we establish the law.

Romans 4:1–5

1. What shall we say then that Abraham our father, as pertaining to the flesh, hath found?
2. For if Abraham were justified by works, he hath whereof to glory; but not before God.
3. For what saith the scripture? Abraham believed God, and it was counted unto him for righteousness.
4. Now to him that worketh is the reward not reckoned of grace, but of debt.

5. But to him that worketh not, but believeth on him that justifieth the ungodly, his faith is counted for righteousness.

Galatians 3:6–9

6. Even as Abraham believed God, and it was accounted to him for righteousness.
7. Know ye therefore that they which are of faith, the same are the children of Abraham.
8. And the scripture, foreseeing that God would justify the heathen through faith, preached before the gospel unto Abraham, saying, In thee shall all nations be blessed.
9. So then they which be of faith are blessed with faithful Abraham.

Paul continues that Abrams righteousness was not just his believe or obedience to God, but he believed in the world redeemer that would come fore as promised by God in

Genesis 3:15

And I will put enmity between thee and the woman, and between thy seed and her seed; it shall bruise thy head, and thou shalt bruise his heel.

GOD PROMISES CANAAN TO ABRAHAM FOR AN INHERITANCE
Genesis 15:7–11

7. *And he said unto him, I am the LORD that brought thee out of Ur of the Chaldees, to give thee this land to inherit it.*
8. *And he said, LORD God, whereby shall I know that I shall inherit it?*
9. *And he said unto him, Take me an heifer of three years old, and a she goat of three years old, and a ram of three years old, and a turtledove, and a young pigeon.*
10. *And he took unto him all these, and divided them in the midst, and laid each piece one against another: but the birds divided he not.*
11. *And when the fowls came down upon the carcases, Abram drove them away.*

How God speaks to Abram "I am the Lord," this is called auto-kerygma [ki-RIG-m*uh*], self-proclamation of God, it is God's declaration of His nature. This phrase is absolute; revealing to man only what and how He chooses.[44]

God explains why He brought Abram out of Ur, "to give thee this land to inherit it." However, Abram is not satisfied and wants assurance he shall inherit. God then instructs him to prepare sacrificial animals in preparation for a formal blood covenant ceremony. The Almighty God directs the animals are to be of three years—why, possibly because the number 3 is sacred and signifies that which is holy. The ancient method of making a covenant was to cut an animal in half, and the contracting parties to pass through the portions of the slain animal, making the parties united by the blood.

Jeremiah 34

18. And I will give the men that have transgressed my covenant, which have not performed the words of the covenant which they had made before me, when they cut the calf in twain, and passed between the parts thereof,

19. The princes of Judah, and the princes of Jerusalem, the eunuchs, and the priests, and all the people of the land, which passed between the parts of the calf.

The birds symbolically represent the obstacles in taking possession of the land, and Abram driving off the birds represent the attempts to frustrate God planes would not succeed.[45]

THE PROMISE CONFIRMED IN A VISION
Genesis 15:12–16

12. *And when the sun was going down, a deep sleep fell upon Abram; and, lo, an horror of great darkness fell upon him.*

13. *And he said unto Abram, Know of a surety that thy seed shall be a stranger in a land that is not theirs, and shall serve them; and they shall afflict them four hundred years;*

---

44   . *The Broadman Commentary*, volume 1, page 164.
45   . *The Pentateuch and Haftorahs*, pages 53–55.

> 14. *And also that nation, whom they shall serve, will I judge: and afterward shall they come out with great substance.*
> 15. *And thou shalt go to thy fathers in peace; thou shalt be buried in a good old age.*
> 16. *But in the fourth generation they shall come hither again: for the iniquity of the Amorites is not yet full.*

God brought a deep sleep onto Abram. The Hebrew[46] is tardemah [tar day maw´], meaning lethargy or trance. These same words are used in the following passages of scripture:

Genesis 2:21

> And the LORD God caused a deep sleep to fall upon Adam, and he slept: and he took one of his ribs, and closed up the flesh instead thereof.

Jobs 4:13

> In thoughts from the visions of the night, when deep sleep falleth on men.

Jobs 33:15

> In a dream, in a vision of the night, when deep sleep falleth upon men, in slumberings upon the bed.

Isaiah 29:10

> For the LORD hath poured out upon you the spirit of deep sleep, and hath closed your eyes: the prophets and your rulers, the seers hath he covered.

With the exception of Genesis 2:21, all the other references are in preparation for a revelation of God. In the following verses, we read an interpretation of the evil omen of verse 11.[47]

These passages are the continuation from the previous visitation in verses 1–6, thus we have in this chapter two nights that the Almighty God appears and provides instruction, and in verses 13–16, Abram is given a glimpse into the future of his descendants. They are to be sojourners in a land that is not theirs and they shall be afflicted for 400 years.

---

46   . James Strong's Hebrew and Chaldee Dictionary of the Old Testament (8639).
47   . *The Interpreters One-Volume Commentary on The Bible* (1971), page 15, Abringdon Press; 201 Eighth Avenue South, Nashville, TN 37203.

Until Joseph brings his brothers and father down into Egypt, Abram's descendants remain in Canaan. The sequence is as follow:

- Abram arrives in Canaan at the age of seventy-five
  Genesis 12:4

    So Abram departed, as the LORD had spoken unto him; and Lot went with him: and Abram was seventy and five years old when he departed out of Haran.

- Isaac is born when Abram is age one hundred
  Genesis 17:1–2, 12
    1. And when Abram was ninety years old and nine, the LORD appeared to Abram, and said unto him, I am the Almighty God; walk before me, and be thou perfect.
    2. Do we then make void the law through faith? God forbid: yea, we establish the law.
    12. Then Abraham fell upon his face, and laughed, and said in his heart, Shall a child be born unto him that is an hundred years old? and shall Sarah, that is ninety years old, bear?

- Jacob is born when Isaac is age sixty
  Genesis 25:26

    And after that came his brother out, and his hand took hold on Esau's heel; and his name was called Jacob: and Isaac was threescore years old when she bare them.

- Jacob and his whole family go down to Egypt at age 130
  Genesis 47:9

    And Jacob said unto Pharaoh, The days of the years of my pilgrimage are an hundred and thirty years: few and evil have the days of the years of my life been, and have not attained unto the days of the years of the life of my fathers in the days of their pilgrimage.

Abram was in Canaan for twenty-five years and had Isaac who was sixty when Jacob was born who was 130 when he entered Egypt; therefore, the sum of the years is 25 + 60 + 130 = 215. According to Exodus, his descendants were in Egypt for 430 years:

Exodus 12:40

> Now the sojourning of the children of Israel, who dwelt in Egypt, was four hundred and thirty years.

That would mean they were in Egypt for 215 years. Abram's descendants would be in bondage for some period, and this was a hash time. After this period, the Hebrews would come out of this bondage as a result of God's judgment upon the Egyptians, and they shall heap treasure upon the children of Abram.

God reveals to Abram he shall have a long life, and when he dies, he shall be with his fathers. This is interest in that he was buried in Canaan, not in Chaldea. This then is an indication of the doctrine of immortality. This doctrine basically states the separation of the spirit and body. The body is mortal, the spirit of man is not; at death the born-again believer enters into the presence of Christ Jesus:[48]

2 Corinthians 5:8

> We are confident, I say, and willing rather to be absent from the body, and to be present with the Lord.

The sting of death has been removed, and the born-again believer falls asleep in Christ Jesus.

1 Corinthians 15:55–57

> 55. O death, where is thy sting? O grave, where is thy victory?
> 56. The sting of death is sin; and the strength of sin is the law.
> 57. But thanks be to God, which giveth us the victory through our Lord Jesus Christ.

1 Thessalonians 4:14

> For if we believe that Jesus died and rose again, even so them also which sleeps in Jesus will God bring with him.

In verse 16, the phrase "the fourth generation" is not a reference to the 400 years, but is the number generation that will be under the yoke of the Egyptians. It is this last

---

48   . *Lectures in Systematic Theology* (1987), pages 337–338, William b. Eerdmans Publishing Company, Grand Rapids, Michigan.

generation that Moses is apart, and they will come out of Egypt and God will direct them against the Amorites. Think of the time God gave the Amorites to repent of their wicked ways.

THE PROMISE CONFIRMED BY A SIGN
Genesis 15:17–21

17. *And it came to pass, that, when the sun went down, and it was dark, behold a smoking furnace, and a burning lamp that passed between those pieces.*
18. *In the same day the LORD made a covenant with Abram, saying, Unto thy seed have I given this land, from the river of Egypt unto the great river, the river Euphrates:*
19. *The Kenites, and the Kenizzites, and the Kadmonites,*
20. *And the Hittites, and the Perizzites, and the Rephaims,*
21. *And the Amorites, and the Canaanites, and the Girgashites, and the Jebusites.*

Once it was dark, God did appear to consummate the formal agreement with Abram. Dr. McGee states we can see Christ Jesus in both the furnace and the lamp. The furnace speaks of judgment and the lamp speaks of Christ Jesus as the light of the world.[49]

Romans 2:16
    In the day when God shall judge the secrets of men by Jesus Christ according to my gospel.

2 Timothy 4:1
    I charge thee therefore before God, and the Lord Jesus Christ, who shall judge the quick and the dead at his appearing and his kingdom.

John 8:12
    Then spake Jesus again unto them, saying, I am the light of the world: he that followeth me shall not walk in darkness, but shall have the light of life.

---

49   . *Thru the Bible*, page 69.

The Blood Covenant[50]

God alone walked through the sacrificed animals, unlike the formal covenant made between men. God has placed no requirement on Abram other than he believes in Him. It is that way today all that is required is to believe on Christ Jesus and what he did on the cross of Calvary.

The remaining verses of this chapter delineate the land of the covenant God has made with Abram. See page 26 for a map depicting the land of promise.

---

50   . http://carefulfornothing.files.wordpress.com/2011/08/
      lahaye1728figures016genxv12abramhasnightmaremed-e1312648745523.jpg?w=334&h=501.

SARAI'S LACK OF FAITH AND ABRAM'S WEAKNESS

Genesis 16

Abram's Counsel to Sarai[51]

CHAPTER OVERVIEW

In this chapter of Genesis, the promise of God that Abram and Sarai shall have a child and be the patriarch and matriarch of vast number offspring reveal the lack of faith by them. Sarai shows her lack of faith, but Abram shows his weakness. Sarai's impatience

---

51   . James Jacques Joseph Tissot (French, 1836–1902), at the Jewish Museum, New York, http://www.thejewishmuseum.org/onlinecollection/object_collection.php?objectid=26685&artistlist=1&an=James.

to have a child coupled with her age, she decides to help God out with His plan and give Hagar her Egyptian maidservant to Abram. Abram should have said no, but he shows his weakness of the flesh.

CHAPTER STRUCTURE

- Sarai plan to have a child via Hagar (1–3)
- Hagar's misbehavior and Sarai response (4–6)
- Hagar's receives instruction from a massager of God (7–14)
- Hagar delivers a son of Abram (15–16)

SARAI'S PLAN TO HAVE A CHILD VIA HAGAR
Genesis 16:1–3

1. *Now Sarai Abram's wife bare him no children: and she had an handmaid, an Egyptian, whose name was Hagar.*
2. *And Sarai said unto Abram, Behold now, the LORD hath restrained me from bearing: I pray thee, go in unto my maid; it may be that I may obtain children by her. And Abram hearkened to the voice of Sarai.*
3. *And Sarai Abram's wife took Hagar her maid the Egyptian, after Abram had dwelt ten years in the land of Canaan, and gave her to her husband Abram to be his wife.*

In verse 1, we are introduced to Sarai's handmaid Hagar. Hagar is of Hebrew origin and means flight or The Sojourner / The Dragged Away One, and there is an Arabic derivation Hajar means forsaken.[52] Hagar is most likely part of the gifts that Pharaoh gave to Abram or the personal slave of Sarai also provided by Pharaoh, and was permitted to leave with her.

Genesis 12:16
> And he entreated Abram well for her sake: and he had sheep, and oxen, and he asses, and menservants, and maidservants, and she asses, and camels.

---

52   , http://www.abarim-publications.com/Meaning/Hagar.html.

Sarai, in her despair over not having a child and presuming to know the mind of God, tells Abram to take Hagar to wife that she could have a child. This is an obsession to the laws of monogamy as defined:

Genesis 2:24

> Therefore shall a man leave his father and his mother, and shall cleave unto his wife: and they shall be one flesh.

This rationale is very foreign to modern sensibilities, but to the culture of the ancient Mideast, this was perfectly acceptable, and even today, this practice continues on the Arabian Peninsula among the Bedouin peoples. Unlike today, a childless couple in the ancient Mideast was considered the woman was cursed by God as a result of sin, and once all the self-examination for sin and the sacrifices completed, they might adopt a son. The husband could take a second wife, he could obtain a son via his concubine, or his wife could do as Sarai has done.[53]

---

53   . *Illustrated Manners and Customs of the Bible* (1980), pages 440–447; Editors James I. Packer,
     Merrill C. Tenney, and William White Jr.; Thomas Nelson Publishers, Nashville, Tennessee.

Sarah presenting Hagar to Abraham[54]

As Hagar is a slave, any child born to her could be considered as a child of Sarai and Abram's house; however, what Sarai had in mind was a bit different. Once Hagar was ready to deliver, Sarai would sit on the birthing stool and Hagar then sit on her lap and as the child entered the world passing through the spread thighs of Sarai symbolically

54 . by Adriaen van der Werff (1659–1722), http://www.deebrestin.com/wp-content/uploads/2010/08/sarah_ fuehrt_abraham_hagar1.jpg.

giving birth; thus she could claim the child as her own.[55] In essence, Hagar would be acting in the role of a surrogate mother.

Abram was complicit in this strategy, and the desires of the flesh had him go along, after all Hagar was a young woman in the midst of her child-bearing years and Abram was in his senior years. However, Abram lost sight of God's promise and plan the son he was to have is of Sarai and himself, but at this point, God had not revealed whom the mother of the child of promise is. Therefore, Abram surely said why not. It is for want of a firm dependence upon God's promise, and patiently waiting for God's timing, that we get in difficulty and make grieves errors in judgment and fall into our sinful nature.[56]

In verse 2, the phrase "*it may be that I may obtain children by her,*" the literal translation of this phrase is, "be builded by her." The rabbinical scholars have interpreted this phrase to mean Sarai would then be said to be Abram's house. That sounds strange to us modern English speakers; however, the Hebrew family is depicted under the image of a house. Sarai would no longer be barren and Abram's house is filled with the joyous noise of a child.[57]

Abram and Sarai commented a sin in the eyes of God. We tend to think it was the fact that Abram is now bigamist and that it was agreeable to Sarai. The sin was their unbelief; For God had said to Abram:

Genesis 12:2
> And I will make of thee a great nation, and I will bless thee, and make thy name great; and thou shalt be a blessing.

No sin is greater or lesser; the difference is in degree the sin of bigamy is just not as black as the sin of unbelief which is a shade lighter. We are all guilty at times of failing in our belief, in Sarai's case, self got in the way. In that culture, a barren woman was a disgrace, and at eighty years of age, she wanted a child of her own. So Hagar would no longer be a slave, but the second wife, but the child would belong to Sarai.

---

55 . *Illustrated Manners and Customs of the Bible* (1980), pages 440–447; Editors James I. Packer, Merrill C. Tenney, and William White Jr.; Thomas Nelson Publishers, Nashville, Tennessee.
56 . Matthew Henry's Commentary; http://www.ewordtoday.com/comments/genesis/mh/genesis16.htm.
57 . *Pentateuch & Haftorahs*, page 56; The Soncino Press Limited, 123 Ditmas Avenue, Brooklyn, New York.

HAGAR'S MISBEHAVIOR AND SARAI'S RESPONSE
Genesis 16:4–6

4. *And he went in unto Hagar, and she conceived: and when she saw that she had conceived, her mistress was despised in her eyes.*

5. *And Sarai said unto Abram, My wrong be upon thee: I have given my maid into thy bosom; and when she saw that she had conceived, I was despised in her eyes: the LORD judge between me and thee.*

6. *But Abram said unto Sarai, Behold, thy maid is in thine hand; do to her as it pleaseth thee. And when Sarai dealt hardly with her, she fled from her face.*

Now Abram is obedient to his wife suggestion and action, and perhaps this is God's plan after all "God helps those who Help themselves." Hagar did conceive; however, she now saw the child she carried as hers; she would not be an incubator for Sarai. As she was now the wife of Abram and no longer the slave, Hagar, basically rubbed Sarai nose in it causing Sarai much anguish:

1 Samuel 1: 6

And her adversary also provoked her sore, for to make her fret, because the LORD had shut up her womb.

As stated in Proverbs, Hagar became hateful and disrespectful of Sarai and saw herself as being superior.[58]

Proverbs 15

1. A soft answer turneth away wrath: but grievous words stir up anger.
2. The tongue of the wise useth knowledge aright: but the mouth of fools poureth out foolishness.

Proverbs 30:23

For an odious woman when she is married; and an handmaid that is heir to her mistress.

---

58   . Broadman, page 167.

Sarai is very distraught over the turn in the situation, goes to her husband, and complains. The complaint was not in what they had done, but that Abram had permitted Sarai to be disrespected by her former handmaiden. Sarai called on God to be the judge of their action, in effect, she was saying, "God, tell this man not to continue permitting my former handmaiden to embarrass and shame me before the people." Abram acted in accordance with those ancient law specifically stated that if a slave elevated to the status of wife could not hold the new position with proper decorum, she was to return to her former position.[59] The unintentional consequences of our sinfulness always come forth in a manner that brings much guilt and grief. Sarai's action of elevating Hagar's status to Abram's wife was motivated by her love and desire to honor her husband's deepest need—a rightful heir. Peter gives the follow admonition:

1 Peter 2:20

> For what glory is it, if, when ye be buffeted for your faults, ye shall take it patiently? but if, when ye do well, and suffer for it, ye take it patiently, this is acceptable with God.

Abram acted with wisdom, and Sarai acted with harshness toward Hagar. Scripture does not stipulate what Sarai's actions were; perhaps whipping, or just worked her very hard. God does not look with favor when the master mistreats a servant:

Job 31

> 13. If I did despise the cause of my manservant or of my maidservant, when they contended with me;
> 14. What then shall I do when God riseth up? and when he visiteth, what shall I answer him?
> 15. Did not he that made me in the womb make him? and did not one fashion us in the womb?

In any case, Hagar, true to her name, ran off. She could no longer endure the harsh treatment she was receiving.

---

59   . Broadman, page 167.

HAGAR RECEIVES INSTRUCTION
FROM A MESSENGER OF GOD
Genesis 16:7–14

7. *And the angel of the LORD found her by a fountain of water in the wilderness, by the fountain in the way to Shur.*
8. *And he said, Hagar, Sarai's maid, whence camest thou? and whither wilt thou go? And she said, I flee from the face of my mistress Sarai.*
9. *And the angel of the LORD said unto her, Return to thy mistress, and submit thyself under her hands.*
10. *And the angel of the LORD said unto her, I will multiply thy seed exceedingly, that it shall not be numbered for multitude.*
11. *And the angel of the LORD said unto her, Behold, thou art with child and shalt bear a son, and shalt call his name Ishmael; because the LORD hath heard thy affliction.*
12. *And he will be a wild man; his hand will be against every man, and every man's hand against him; and he shall dwell in the presence of all his brethren.*
13. *And she called the name of the LORD that spake unto her, Thou God seest me: for she said, Have I also here looked after him that seeth me?*
14. *Wherefore the well was called Beerlahairoi; behold, it is between Kadesh and Bered.*

HAGAR'S CONVERSATION WITH GOD
Verses 7–10

In this passage is the first mention of angel in the Bible. However this is no ordinary angel, meaning messenger of God. Hagar is conversing with God as apparent by verse 10, "*I will multiply thy seed exceedingly.*" When one reads the "angel of the LORD," the capitalization indicates God and is referred to as a theophany or Christophe—Christ Jesus per incarnation.

Map of Shur Desert[60]

Shur means an enclosure, a wall, a part, probably, of the Arabian desert, on the northeastern border of Egypt, giving its name to a wilderness extending from Egypt toward Philistia. The name was probably given to it from the wall (or shur) which the Egyptians built to defend their frontier on the northeast from the desert tribes. This wall or line of fortifications extended from Pelusium to Heliopolisa.

Doctor Hertz states that verse 7 is a wonderful illustration of the divine regard for the forlorn and desolate soul. The Lord found her; the inference is the Lord stopped her at the fountain. It is obvious Hagar was fleeing to her homeland—Egypt.

The two questions put to her by the angel of the Lord are at the heart of human existence: (1) Where have you come from? and (2) Where are you going? Her answer to the first should have affected her understanding of the second. Whenever we attempt to determine who we are and the direction we are planning for the future, we must not ignore our origins. For Hagar to cut off her past as she faced the future was to miss

---

60   . http://www.israel-a-history-of.com/hagar.html.

her destiny. She is commanded to return whence she came and to submit herself to her mistress. In so doing, she will define her relationship and her place in history.[61]

HAGAR RECEIVES REVELATION
Verses 11–14

The Lord then tells her she will have a son and his name shall be Ishmael [God listens] and he will multiply his descendants because the Lord heard her affliction. The Ishmaelite is the ancestors of the Arabians and they often refer to themselves as his children, as well as Abu Abraham. God then relates to her the character and manner of her son and his prodigy. God states he will be a wild man; the wild ass of the Arabian deserts was a noble creature, and a fine symbol of the free-roving life of the Arab.

Job 39

4. Who hath sent out the wild ass free? or who hath loosed the bands of the wild ass?
5. Whose house I have made the wilderness, and the barren land his dwellings.
6. He scorneth the multitude of the city, neither regardeth he the crying of the driver.
7. The range of the mountains is his pasture, and he searcheth after every green thing.

He shall dwell in the presence of all his brethren. This is an idiomatic use of the Hebrew "al penē" (literally, "upon/against the face of"). More particularly, it means "in defiance/disregard of," as proved by:

Deuteronomy 21:16

Then it shall be, when he maketh his sons to inherit that which he hath, that he may not make the son of the beloved firstborn before the son of the hated, which is indeed the firstborn.

Genesis 25:18

And they dwelt from Havilah unto Shur that is before Egypt, as thou goest toward Assyria: and he died in the presence of all his brethren.

---

61   . Broadman, volume 1, page 168.

Thus the idiom and context denote hostility on the part of Ishmael and his descendants against his brethren Isaac and his descendants.[62] Today we can observe the truth in the above, for the Ishmaelite/Arabs have been making war on their brothers, the Israelites. The intensity will only increase the closer we get to the return of Christ Jesus.

Verses 13 and 14 are most interesting in that they deal with the name of this fountain. *Thou God seest me*, Hebrew 'Ēl Rái, meaning a God of seeing or a God vision. This means not so much a God who sees as a God who permits Himself to be seen. Hagar's comment *"Have I also here looked after him that seeth me?"* is equally diffcult to translate and possibly means, "Have I seen God and survived?"[63] From the following scripture, the reader will note that one looking on the Face of God shall die.

Exodus 33
20. And he said, I will make all my goodness pass before thee, and I will proclaim the name of the LORD before thee; and will be gracious to whom I will be gracious, and will shew mercy on whom I will shew mercy.
21. And he said, Thou canst not see my face: for there shall no man see me, and live.

Therefore, the name of the well is Beerlahairoi [be-ayr' lakh-ah'ee ro-ee'][64] and may be translated as "well of the living/seeing," transliteration "well of continuing to live after seeing God." That a human should be allowed to see God and live is a mark of special honor favor,[65] as depicted in the following scriptures:

Genesis 32:30
And Jacob called the name of the place Peniel: for I have seen God face to face, and my life is preserved.

Exodus 3:6
Moreover he said, I am the God of thy father, the God of Abraham, the God of Isaac, and the God of Jacob. And Moses hid his face; for he was afraid to look upon God.

---

62 . *The Parallel Bible Commentary*, page 51.
63 . *The Parallel Bible Commentary*, page 51.
64 . The Old Testament Hebrew Lexicon; http://www.searchgodsword.org/lex/heb/view.cgi?number=0883.
65 . *The Parallel Bible Commentary*, page 51.

HAGAR DELIVERS A SON OF ABRAM
Genesis 16:15–16

15. And Hagar bare Abram a son: and Abram called his son's name, which Hagar bare, Ishmael.

16. And Abram was fourscore and six years old, when Hagar bare Ishmael to Abram.

It is obvious that Hagar returned to Sarai her mistress and gave birth to her and Abram's son, Ishmael, as God had commended. Abram is now eighty-six, and thirteen more years will pass before God once again speaks to him about a son of his and Sarai—the son of promise.

God Renews His Promise to Abram

Genesis 17

God Renews Promises to Abram[66]

CHAPTER OVERVIEW

Thirteen years have passed since the birth of Ishmael, and God appears before Abram and renews His covenant with him to inherit the land and that he shall be the father of many nations. God commands as a sign of this covenant between them, the circumcision of all males of his house. God gives Abram and his wife, Sarai, new names. God bless

66   . by James Jacques Joseph Tissot (French, 1836–1902), at the Jewish Museum, New York, http://www.
        thejewishmuseum.org/onlinecollection/object_collection.php?objectid=26688&artistlist=1&an=James.

Ishmael, but the covenant is for and with the son of promise, and his descendants. The chapter ends with the execution of God's command, the circumcision of all males.

CHAPTER STRUCTURE

- God Appears as El Shaddai (1–3)
- God Gives Abram a New Name (4–8)
- Token of the Covenant (9–14)
- God Gives Sarai a New Name (15–19)
- Blessing of Ishmael (20–21)
- God Departs and the Execution Token (22–27)

GOD APPEARS AS EL SHADDAI
Genesis 17:1–3

1. *And when Abram was ninety years old and nine, the LORD appeared to Abram, and said unto him, I am the Almighty God; walk before me, and be thou perfect.*
2. *And I will make my covenant between me and thee, and will multiply thee exceedingly.*
3. *And Abram fell on his face: and God talked with him, saying,*

In chapter 16, when Abram was eighty-six, the birth of Ishmael has occurred, and God once again appears to Abram after thirteen years have elapsed. Perhaps Abram though of Ishmael as the son of promise, and Sarai had the correct interpretation of God's plan, but is this why the absence of God the last thirteen years? When we presume to know the mind of God, we fall into sin, and in Sarai's case, it is the lack of faith.

In a way, she symbolizes the tome of Christ Jesus, for like the tome which only houses death, the womb of Sarai is dead. However, this is about to change, and just as Christ Jesus came forth for the tome, so to Sarah's womb will bring forth life.[67] Paul writes in:

---

67   . *Thru the Bible*, volume 1, page 73.

Romans 4:19

> And being not weak in faith, he considered not his own body now dead, when he was about an hundred years old, neither yet the deadness of Sarah's womb.

And Paul concludes the fourth chapter thusly:

Romans 4:25

> Who was delivered for our offenses, and was raised again for our justification.

God announces Himself with a new name: *I am the Almighty God.* The Hebrew for Almighty is El-Shaddai: the El is translated God and appears 229 times in the King James Bible and is the root for the more frequently used Elohiym and appears 2,591 times in the Old Testament. El means the strong and mighty one.[68] Shaddai is derived from the Hebrew word *Shad* meaning breast, which signifies Shaddai is one that nourishes, supplies, and satisfies, or the All Sufficient God. For it is God that supplies all our needs and bless us with children, which is the usage of El Shaddai and appears 48 time in the Bible, and when used with the Patriarchs, there is the phrase *will multiply thee* indicating God's blessing of children.

Genesis 28:3

> And God Almighty bless thee, and make thee fruitful, and multiply thee, that thou mayest be a multitude of people.

Genesis 35:11

> And God said unto him, I am God Almighty: be fruitful and multiply; a nation and a company of nations shall be of thee, and kings shall come out of thy loins.

Genesis 48:3–4

> 3. And Jacob said unto Joseph, God Almighty appeared unto me at Luz in the land of Canaan, and blessed me,
> 4. And said unto me, Behold, I will make thee fruitful, and multiply thee, and I will make of thee a multitude of people; and will give this land to thy seed after thee for an everlasting possession.

---

68   . http://www.lifetv.org/Web_IITML/html/Commentary%20folderfolder/El_Shaddai.htm.

Genesis 49:25

> Even by the God of thy father, who shall help thee; and by the Almighty, who shall bless thee with blessings of heaven above, blessings of the deep that lieth under, blessings of the breasts, and of the womb.

El Shaddai is used almost exclusively in reference to the patriarchs—Abraham, Isaac, and Jacob—and was the primary name by which God was known to the founders of Israel.[69]

Exodus 6:2–3

> 2. And God spake unto Moses, and said unto him, I am the LORD:
> 3. And I appeared unto Abraham, unto Isaac, and unto Jacob, by the name of God Almighty, but by my name JEHOVAH was I not known to them.

Most English translations render El Shaddai as God Almighty, most likely because the translators of the Septuagint (the Greek translation of the Old Testament) translated Shaddai using the Greek word "pantokrator," "Almighty," the "One who has is hand on everything." However, the root word "shadad" means to "overpower" or "to destroy." Therefore, St. Jerome (writer, linguist, and translator of original biblical text into the Latin Vulgate) translated Shaddai as "Omnipotens" or the English omnipotent. God is so overpowering that he is considered "Almighty."[70]

There is one final point to make before moving on to the next item of discussion. It is from the names of God that we learn who God is. We learn the who and the what of God's characteristic attributes. God is, in a word, awesome!

God tells Abram to *walk before me, and be thou perfect*. Isn't it interesting that God would say walk before me? God walk with Enoch and Noah:

Genesis 5:24

> And Enoch walked with God: and he was not; for God took him.

---

69   . http://www.hebrew4christians.com/Names_of_G-d/El.
70   . http://www.hebrew4christians.com/Names_of_G-d/El.

Genesis 6:9

> These are the generations of Noah: Noah was a just man and perfect in his generations, and Noah walked with God.

However, Abram is told to walk before God. One may ask why, if Abram is chosen of God and has a covenant with God, why the walk before? The obvious answer: Abram and Sarai's lack of faith, with regard to their having a child, Sarai gave Hagar her handmaiden to Abram to have a child. How God is telling Abram to be before him, but it is that last part of God's command that is the challenge, be thou perfect.

The word *perfect* is from the Hebrew "tamiym" and means without blemish, complete, integrity, sincerity, without spot, undefiled.[71] As can be seen, does anyone comply with this list of requirements? This can only be accomplished via the blood of Christ Jesus and the Holy Spirit working within us. In Abram's case, he could not permit his faith to falter and rely on Almighty God to keep Him on track. The implication is not moral perfect, but a complete and undeniable devotion to God.

Deuteronomy 18:13

> Thou shalt be perfect with the LORD thy God.

Abram's challenge is to give himself to serve God without reservation or ulterior motive. He is to conduct himself in complete obedience before God.

Deuteronomy 10:12

> And now, Israel, what doth the LORD thy God require of thee, but to fear the LORD thy God, to walk in all his ways, and to love him, and to serve the LORD thy God with all thy heart and with all thy soul.

Micah 6:8

> He hath shewed thee, O man, what is good; and what doth the LORD require of thee, but to do justly, and to love mercy, and to walk humbly with thy God?

---

71   . *Hebrew-Greek Key Word Study Bible* (1991); AMG Publishers, Chattanooga, Tennessee.

God once again states the covenant is between Himself, Abram, and his descendants. Some twenty-four years had passed since God made the blood covenant with Abram, Genesis 15, and now renews it.

Abram's response to this theophany is to fall on his face. With this demonstration of great humility and abject submission, Abram prostrates himself before God. For Abram looked upon himself as merely the creature far below the creator-God, and upon God with fear and awe, thus the posture of adoration.

God graciously condescend to communicate with who He has established a covenant. God continues to speak with His children (saints, born-again believers) by His word, the Bible:

Proverbs 6:22

> When thou goest, it shall lead thee; when thou sleepest, it shall keep thee; and when thou awakest, it shall talk with thee.

And by His Holy Spirit:

John 14:26

> But the Comforter, which is the Holy Ghost, whom the Father will send in my name, he shall teach you all things, and bring all things to your remembrance, whatsoever I have said unto you.

If we are to have fellowship with God Almighty, we must be of a humble heart and approach him with reverence. However, if there is contempt resulting from familiarity, we deceive ourselves for we are not born-again-believers. When we worship at God's footstool and give Him praise and glory, then His Holy Spirit shall comfort us.[72]

GOD GIVES ABRAM A NEW NAME
Genesis 17:4–8

4. *As for me, behold, my covenant is with thee, and thou shalt be a father of many nations.*

---

72   . Matthew Henry's Commentary, volume 1, page 89.

5. *Neither shall thy name any more be called Abram, but thy name shall be Abraham; for a father of many nations have I made thee.*

6. *And I will make thee exceeding fruitful, and I will make nations of thee, and kings shall come out of thee.*

7. *And I will establish my covenant between me and thee and thy seed after thee in their generations for an everlasting covenant, to be a God unto thee, and to thy seed after thee.*

8. *And I will give unto thee, and to thy seed after thee, the land wherein thou art a stranger, all the land of Canaan, for an everlasting possession; and I will be their God.*

As a part of the covenant God now gives Abram (meaning "high father" or "father of the height" or "exalted father") a new name, from this point forward he will be known as Abraham meaning "father of a multitude" or "father of many nation." The nobility confers titles on their favorites to dignify them, so to God has dignified Abraham with the new name. Unlike today, a person's name was significant as it conveyed information about the person. Actually, all believers will receive a new name.

Revelation 2:17

He that hath an ear, let him hear what the Spirit saith unto the churches; To him that overcometh will I give to eat of the hidden manna, and will give him a white stone, and in the stone a new name written, which no man knoweth saving he that receiveth it.

Imagine having a name that meant high father and you have no children; this must be the cause of some remorse and pain. Once again God has appeared and has changed his name to the father of multitude and promised him more descendants than one can count. Abraham had to have much happiness. The fact is Abraham is the father of a multitude, his descendants live around the world. Isaac's (Hebrews) and Ishmael's (Arabs) descendants become the head of state and are a vast people; on top of that, add in all of Abraham's spiritual seed (born-again believers) by faith in Christ Jesus.

Romans 4:16

Therefore it is of faith, that it might be by grace; to the end the promise might be sure to all the seed; not to that only which is of the law, but to that also which is of the faith of Abraham; who is the father of us all.

God is omnipresent and omnipotent; He knows our future and speak of it in our present, as in the case of Abram, now Abraham. We have a tendency to speak our past into our future, but God speaks our future into the present.

Romans 4:17

> (As it is written, I have made thee a father of many nations,) before him whom he believed, even God, who quickeneth the dead, and calleth those things which be not as though they were.

In verses 7 and 8, God reiterates his covenant as though Abraham will be there when it all takes place. Today the Hebrews only control a small strip of the Promised Land, but in the day of the Lord, they are going to control all that God promised.

TOKEN OF THE COVENANT[73]
Genesis 17:9–14

9. *And God said unto Abraham, Thou shalt keep my covenant therefore, thou, and thy seed after thee in their generations.*
10. *This is my covenant, which ye shall keep, between me and you and thy seed after thee; Every man child among you shall be circumcised.*
11. *And ye shall circumcise the flesh of your foreskin; and it shall be a token of the covenant betwixt me and you.*
12. *And he that is eight days old shall be circumcised among you, every man child in your generations, he that is born in the house, or bought with money of any stranger, which is not of thy seed.*
13. *He that is born in thy house, and he that is bought with thy money, must needs be circumcised: and my covenant shall be in your flesh for an everlasting covenant.*
14. *And the uncircumcised man child whose flesh of his foreskin is not circumcised, that soul shall be cut off from his people; he hath broken my covenant.*

The token of the covenant is the circumcision of all the males of the house of Abraham, no matter free or slave. The scriptures call this promise of God the covenant of circumcision, Acts 7:8:

---

73   . All of this section is taken from Matthew Henry's commentary, volume 1, page 91. With a few exception of my own commentary, but the bulk of it is Matthew Henry's.

And he gave him the covenant of circumcision: and so Abraham begat Isaac, and circumcised him the eighth day; and Isaac begat Jacob; and Jacob begat the twelve patriarchs.

Circumcision is the emblem of the covenant, which scripture calls a sign and seal:

Romans 4:11
> And he received the sign of circumcision, a seal of the righteousness of the faith which he had yet being uncircumcised: that he might be the father of all them that believe, though they be not circumcised; that righteousness might be imputed unto them also:

It is an affirmation to Abraham and his progeny of those promises which are God's haft of the covenant. Further, they are to observe all that God commands, in effect they are debtors to the law.

Galatians 5:3
> For I testify again to every man that is circumcised, that he is a debtor to do the whole law.

This is a bloody ordinance; for all things are purged with blood in accordance with the law, Hebrews 9:22:
> And almost all things are by the law purged with blood; and without shedding of blood is no remission.

Exodus 24:8
> And Moses took the blood, and sprinkled it on the people, and said, Behold the blood of the covenant, which the LORD hath made with you concerning all these words.

However, the shed blood of Christ Jesus put an end to this ordinance; circumcision gave way to baptism. Nevertheless, it is not the act of baptism that brings on salvation; just as the act of circumcision does not bring salvation. In Abraham's time, it was faith in God and obedience to His law. However, since Calvary and the work Christ Jesus did there to redeem the sinner, the significance of circumcision for the believer is relegated to a health issue, not a salvation issue. We must now accept Christ Jesus as our Lord and savior, in effect to be born again:

John 3:5–7
5. Jesus answered, Verily, verily, I say unto thee, Except a man be born of water and of the Spirit, he cannot enter into the kingdom of God.
6. That which is born of the flesh is flesh; and that which is born of the Spirit is spirit.
7. Marvel not that I said unto thee, Ye must be born again.

There are those that question, what of women in this covenant and does she have a part? Women, child and adult, must be definitely covered by the covenant, for the man covers her, as Christ Jesus covers the church:

Ephesians 5:23–25
23. For the husband is the head of the wife, even as Christ is the head of the church: and he is the savior of the body.
24. Therefore as the church is subject unto Christ, so let the wives be to their own husbands in every thing.
25. Husbands, love your wives, even as Christ also loved the church, and gave himself for it;

Sin propagates by each successive generation; therefore, God would require of man in entering into this covenant the offering of his foreskin. It is a secret part of the body; for true circumcision is of the heart: this honor God put upon an uncomely part.

1 Corinthians 12:23–24
23. And those members of the body, which we think to be less honorable, upon these we bestow more abundant honor; and our uncomely parts have more abundant comeliness.
24. For our comely parts have no need: but God hath tempered the body together, having given more abundant honor to that part which lacked.

On the eighth day of the baby boy's life, the execution of ordinance occurs. It is on this day that newborns have more antibodies and can resist infection. Matthew Henry put it this way: "They might gather some strength; to be able to undergo the pain of it, and that at least one Sabbath might past over them."

In verses 12 and 13, God addresses the strangers or slave of Abraham's house. These are of the Gentiles, although they were bought with money; the Christian is redeemed by the blood of Christ Jesus. It is by faith that we are also partakers of the promises of God.

Galatians 3:14
> That the blessing of Abraham might come on the Gentiles through Jesus Christ; that we might receive the promise of the Spirit through faith.

Verse 14 speaks of the penalty for not executing the covenant. This is a contemptuous act of disobedience, which God deals with severely. It is a dangerous thing to make light of divine institutions and to live in the neglect of them. Moses is a good example:

Exodus 4:24–26
> 24. And it came to pass by the way in the inn, that the LORD met him, and sought to kill him.
> 25. Then Zipporah took a sharp stone, and cut off the foreskin of her son, and cast it at his feet, and said, Surely a bloody husband art thou to me.
> 26. So he let him go: then she said, A bloody husband thou art, because of the circumcision.

GOD GIVES SARAI A NEW NAME
Genesis 17:15–19

> 15. *And God said unto Abraham, As for Sarai thy wife, thou shalt not call her name Sarai, but Sarah shall her name be.*
> 16. *And I will bless her, and give thee a son also of her: yea, I will bless her, and she shall be a mother of nations; kings of people shall be of her.*
> 17. *Then Abraham fell upon his face, and laughed, and said in his heart, Shall a child be born unto him that is an hundred years old? and shall Sarah, that is ninety years old, bear?*
> 18. *And Abraham said unto God, O that Ishmael might live before thee!*

19. And God said, Sarah thy wife shall bear thee a son indeed; and thou shalt call his name Isaac: and I will establish my covenant with him for an everlasting covenant, and with his seed after him.

Just as God gave Abraham, so to dignify Sarai (meaning my princess) with the name of Sarah (meaning princess), as Sarai she is the princess of Abram only. Now as Sarah, she is princess of the multitude of peoples and from her womb the King of kings shall come fore.

Both Sarah and Abraham dignified by the addition of a single letter to their names, and that letter is **H**. That H comes from the name of God "JeHovaH," and this is the matter in which God chose to honor them. It is hard for us to comprehend the significance of the sharing of a single letter, because many names share the same letter. To the ancient world, this sharing carried great honor; it is as though a king would bestow the title upon an individual who had never possessed one.

For the first time Abraham is told Sarah will conceive and bear him a son. Upon hearing this, he fall on his face in worship and adoration. The laughter of Abraham has brought about to two schools of thought: one of unbelief, because of his and Sarah's age and in verse 18 he asks about Ishmael. The other sees the laughter as of joy, and not disbelief, in the words of J. Vernon McGee: "Abraham believed in God, and he is absolutely overwhelmed by the wonder and the goodness of God." Paul in his epistle to the Romans 4:17–22:

17. (As it is written, I have made thee a father of many nations,) before him whom he believed, even God, who quickeneth the dead, and calleth those things which be not as though they were.
18. Who against hope believed in hope, that he might become the father of many nations, according to that which was spoken, So shall thy seed be.
19. And being not weak in faith, he considered not his own body now dead, when he was about an hundred years old, neither yet the deadness of Sarah's womb:
20. He staggered not at the promise of God through unbelief; but was strong in faith, giving glory to God;
21. And being fully persuaded that, what he had promised, he was able also to perform.
22. And therefore it was imputed to him for righteousness.

In verse 18, Abraham asks of his son with Hagar, that God not forget about him. Ishmael is thirteen years of age and Abraham loves him. Over the years, Abraham must have had regret for taken Hagar to wife. The jealousy of the two mothers will reappear, and by chapter 21, it will come to a head. This is the result of their sin, and it continues to manifest itself in that region of the world, as illuminated by the Israelis and Palestines, which is now overflowing into the rest of the world, because of the sin of Abraham and Sarah. Paul in his epistle Galatians 6:7:

> Be not deceived; God is not mocked: for whatsoever a man soweth, that shall he also reap.

Verse 19 is the denial of Abraham's request to think of Ishmael for the promise. Like any parent, Abraham only wanted the best for Ishmael. God tells Abraham that the son of promise is named Isaac (meaning laugher[74]), and it is with him that God will make the everlasting covenant and to his son. His name will serve as a reminder that God keeps His promise and of the unlikely means by which he came into the world.[75]

BLESSING OF ISHMAEL
Genesis 17:20–21

> 20. *And as for Ishmael, I have heard thee: Behold, I have blessed him, and will make him fruitful, and will multiply him exceedingly; twelve princes shall he beget, and I will make him a great nation.*
> 21. *But my covenant will I establish with Isaac, which Sarah shall bear unto thee at this set time in the next year.*

God reassures Abraham that he did not forget about Ishmael. God has blessed him, and he will be the father of twelve princes and make of him a great nation. These twelve princes are namely:

Genesis 25:13–15
> 13. And these are the names of the sons of Ishmael, by their names, according to their generations: the firstborn of Ishmael, Nebajoth; and Kedar, and Adbeel, and Mibsam,

---

74   . Nelson's New Illustrated Bible Dictionary, page 604.
75   . The Parallel Bible Commentary, page 52.

14 Who against hope believed in hope, that he might become the father of many nations, according to that which was spoken, So shall thy seed be.

15. Hadar, and Tema, Jetur, Naphish, and Kedemah.

Nations of Ishmael's Son[76]

Adbeel [AD bee el] – Ishmael's third son, and name of an Arabian tribe located in northwest Arabia

Dumah [Dew mah] – Ishmael's sixth son
- a. ancestor of an Arabian tribe (1 Chr. 1:3)
- b. A town in the hill country of Judah (Josh. 15:52). Moderned – Domeh, about 8 miles southwest of Hebron.
- c. A symbolic name of Edom, or a place in Arabia (Is. 21:11)

Hadar [Hay dahr] - Ishmael's eighth son
- a. Also known as Hadad [Hay dad]
- b. City of Edom (1 Chr. 1:30)

Jetur [JEE tuhr] – Ishmael's tenth son

His tribe warred against the tribes of Reuben and Gad and with the haft-tribe of Manasseh (1 Chr. 5:19)

Kedar [KEE dur] – Ishmael's second son

A region of northern Arabian desert and inhabited by tribe bearing the same name (Isa. 21:15–17)

Kedemah [KED eh muh] – Ishmael's twelfth son

Name of Arabian tribe (1 Chr. 1:31)

Massa [MASS uh] – Ishmael's son

Founder of an Arabian tribe, known as Masani

Occupy a region near the Persian Gulf

Mibsam [MIB sam] – Ishmael's son

Mishma [MISH muh] – Ishmael's son

Became an Arabian tribe

Naphish [NAY fish] – Ishmael's son

Founder of the clam on the east side of the Jordan River

The Israelites were victorious over them (1 Chr. 5:19)

Nebajoth [neh Bay yoth] – Ishmael's first son

Ancestor of Arabian tribe that bears his name (Is. 60:7)

76   . Nelson's New Illustrated Bible Dictionary, pages 21, 370, 530, 673, 724, 808, 829, 849, 880, 885, and 1230.

Tema [TEE muh] - Ishmael's ninth son

> Name of a desert city in northwest Arabia, about midway between
> Babylon and Egypt (Job 6:19; Is. 21:14; Jer. 25:23)
> Present-day Teima

Ishmael's sons settled

Abraham is told Isaac will be born the same time next year, and the covenant will pass
on to him and his descendants after him. God chose whom He pleases into a covenant

with Himself. It is according to the will and pleasure of God, not our will! For it is written in scriptures:

Malachi 1:2–3
2   I have loved you, saith the LORD. Yet ye say, Wherein hast thou loved us? Was not Esau Jacob's brother? saith the LORD: yet I loved Jacob,

3   And I hated Esau, and laid his mountains and his heritage waste for the dragons of the wilderness.

Romans 9:8, 13, 18
8.   That is, They which are the children of the flesh, these are not the children of God: but the children of the promise are counted for the seed.

13. As it is written, Jacob have I loved, but Esau have I hated.

18. Therefore hath he mercy on whom he will have mercy, and whom he will he hardeneth.

It may have broken Abraham's heart that Ishmael was not the son of promise; it is all about God. Even today the Holy Spirit call some to be salvation and repentance and others He does not.

GOD DEPARTS AND THE TOKEN IS EXECUTED
Genesis 22–27

22. *And he left off talking with him, and God went up from Abraham.*
23. *And Abraham took Ishmael his son, and all that were born in his house, and all that were bought with his money, every male among the men of Abraham's house; and circumcised the flesh of their foreskin in the selfsame day, as God had said unto him.*
24. *And Abraham was ninety years old and nine, when he was circumcised in the flesh of his foreskin.*
25. *And Ishmael his son was thirteen years old, when he was circumcised in the flesh of his foreskin.*
26. *In the selfsame day was Abraham circumcised, and Ishmael his son.*
27. *And all the men of his house, born in the house, and bought with money of the stranger, were circumcised with him.*

The business of the circumcision of covenant is now complete and all parties know their requirements. With the business concluded, God now departs. One day we will be able to converse with God face-to-face not receiving direction and instruction, but the pure joy of being in His presence, an everlasting feast.[77]

It was an implicit obedience: Abraham did as God said to him and did not ask why or wherefore. God's will was not only a law to him, but a reason; he did it because God told him. It was speedy and sincere obedience not dilatory. As the writer of Psalms states:

Psalms 119:60
    I made haste, and delayed not to keep thy commandments.

It was a universal obedience; Abraham desired that all his might share with him in it. Though God's covenant was not established with Ishmael, he was circumcised. Ishmael is blessed and therefore circumcised.

Note:
    This is where many of the main line denomination (Lutheran, Presbyterian, Anglican, Catholic, etc.) get the baptism of infants and very young children. The parents are believers, as such have the right to the privileges of having child made part of the visible church, and the seal of the new covenant, whatever they may prove afterward.

    The thinking is this: as a believer (a member of the invisible church), being baptized makes the believer a member of the visible church. Every believer wants their children to be born again and baptized. The children are not at a point of understanding yet, but they can be members of the visible church by being baptized into the faith.

    This thinking has led many a young person astray, thinking they are born-again believers. That their sin has been washed away by the water, and this is totally false. Let's look to scripture:

---

77   . This section is taken from Matthew Henry's Commentary, volume 1, page 92.

John 3:5–6
1. Jesus answered, "Most assuredly, I say to you, unless one is born of water and the Spirit, he cannot enter the kingdom of God.
2. That which is born of the flesh is flesh, and that which is born of the Spirit is spirit.

These passages mean being born of water is the natural birth, and being born of the Spirit is altogether different as scripture states:

Romans 10:9–10
9. That if you confess with your mouth the Lord Jesus and believe in your heart that God has raised Him from the dead, you will be saved.
10. For with the heart one believes unto righteousness, and with the mouth confession is made unto salvation.

If one would make a most simple prayer, asking God the Father to forgive our sins by the name of Christ Jesus, you will be "saved" born again.

1 John 1:9
If we confess our sins, He is faithful and just to forgive us *our* sins and to cleanse us from all unrighteousness.

Circumcision is painful, and for grown men shamful, while in this condition of being sore and unfit to defend themselve against attack, as Simeon and Levi did against the Shechemites. Abraham being ninety-nine years of age is such a strange thing done religiously and might be a reproach by their neighbors, the Canaanites and Perizzites. Yet the command God is sufficient to answer a thousand such objection. What is required by God we must comply, and not confer with other people about the command.

Circumcision of Ishmael[78]

Note:

> The Arabians circumcize the boy at puberty or at age thirteen, in emulation
> of Ishmael. In the Aser region of Saudi Arabia, which is located in the
> southeast along the Red Sea, they have a very public ceremony. The boy of the
> village are lined up, that is correct standing, and their eldest sister is required
> to cut away the foreskin, and all the while he is to sing her praises; if there
> is no elder sister, then one of the boy's elder female cousins or some female
> family member.

78   . Illustrators of the 1728 *Figures de la Bible*, Gerard Hoet (1648–1733), published by P. de Hondt in The Hague in
        1728;   http://www.mythfolklore.net/lahaye/017/LaHaye1728Figures01/GenXVII23AbramCircumcisesIsmael.
        jpg.

ABRAHAM'S ENTERTAINMENT OF ANGELS

Genesis 18

Abraham and the Three Angels[79]

---

79   . James Jacques Joseph Tissot (French, 1836–1902); *Abraham and the Three Angels*, c. 1896–1902, http://www. thejewishmuseum.org/onlinecollection/object_collection.php?objectid=26696&lefttxt=James Jacques Joseph Tissot.

CHAPTER OVERVIEW

We have an account in this chapter of another interview between God and Abraham, probably within a few days after the former, as a reward of his cheerful obedience to the law of circumcision. Here is the visit that God made him, and the kind entertainment that he gave to that visit. The matters discoursed of between them are the purposes of God's love concerning Sarah, and the purposes of God's wrath concerning Sodom. The discovery God made to Abraham of his design to destroy Sodom, and the intercession Abraham made for Sodom.

CHAPTER STRUCTURE

- The Lord appears to Abraham. (1–8)
- Sarah's unbelief reproved. (9–15)
- God reveals the destruction of Sodom. (16–22)
- Abraham's intercession for Sodom. (23–33)

THE LORD APPEARS TO ABRAHAM
Genesis 18:1–8

1. *And the LORD appeared unto him in the plains of Mamre: and he sat in the tent door in the heat of the day;*
2. *And he lift up his eyes and looked, and, lo, three men stood by him: and when he saw them, he ran to meet them from the tent door, and bowed himself toward the ground,*
3. *And said, My LORD, if now I have found favor in thy sight, pass not away, I pray thee, from thy servant:*
4. *Let a little water, I pray you, be fetched, and wash your feet, and rest yourselves under the tree:*
5. *And I will fetch a morsel of bread, and comfort ye your hearts; after that ye shall pass on: for therefore are ye come to your servant. And they said, So do, as thou hast said.*
6. *And Abraham hastened into the tent unto Sarah, and said, Make ready quickly three measures of fine meal, knead it, and make cakes upon the hearth.*

7. *And Abraham ran unto the herd, and fetcht a calf tender and good, and gave it unto a young man; and he hasted to dress it.*

8. *And he took butter, and milk, and the calf which he had dressed, and set it before them; and he stood by them under the tree, and they did eat.*

And the LORD appeared unto him. The rabbinical scholars connect this chapter with the preceding and declare that God visited Abraham during the indisposition resulting from the circumcision, God came to heal him. It is from this passage the rabbis deduce the duty of visiting the sick.[80]

From verse 1, we know that it is late afternoon for that is when the heat of the day occurs, approximately 4:00 PM (*post meridiem)*, and Abraham had pitched his tent on the plains of Mamre, see map on page 153, which is by Hebron.

Genesis 13:18

Then Abram removed his tent, and came and dwelt in the plain of Mamre, which is in Hebron, and built there an altar unto the LORD.

Abraham saw the three men approaching and ran to greet them, entreating them to stay with him that he might entertain them. The hospitality he exhibited reflects his love of God as manifested in his desire to serve others. Abraham was waiting to entertain any weary travelers, for inns were not available as today. Also the statement in the following:

Deuteronomy 10:19

Love ye therefore the stranger: for ye were strangers in the land of Egypt.

Hebrews 13:2

Be not forgetful to entertain strangers: for thereby some have entertained angels unawares.

Who are these three men? Dr. Lightfoot suggests they represent the Trinity, but this is an incorrect assertion. They are the Lord Christ Jesus and two attending angels. In

---

80 . *Pentateuch & Haftorahs*, page 63.

this visitation of Abraham occurrence is a Christophany, which is Christ Jesus appears incarnate prior to his earthly ministry commencement.

John 3:13

> And no man hath ascended up to heaven, but he that came down from heaven, even the Son of man which is in heaven.

The rabbinical scholars' state in the Midrash, an angel is never sent on more than one errand at a time. Therefore, the first anglel is to announce the birth of Isaac; the second angel is to destroy Sodom; and the third angel is to rescue Lot.[81]

In addition, in verse 2, "*bowed himself toward the ground*," he prostrated himself before them, a sign of reverence and submission. Abraham addressed one of them as "*My LORD*" from the Hebrew text "*Adonai*," the Old Testament term used for God exclusively.[82] He knew clearly he was face to face with his and our creator; therefore, he acted accordingly.

The indication that Abraham recognized them as who they are, Abraham in the preparation of the meal, has a fatted calf prepared, cakes made by Sarah served with milk and butter. Had they been normal travelers, the feast would not have had Sarah involved in the preparation and there would be no meat. More than likely, the meal would consist of honey, dates, and tea/water/maybe milk.

"*wash your feet*" This is the first reference made of foot washing in the Bible. The root of this practice appears to be found in the hospitality customs of ancient civilizations, especially where sandals were the chief footwear. A host would provide water for guests to wash their feet, provide a servant to wash the feet of the guests, or even serve the guests by washing their feet. It is found in the following scriptures:

Genesis 19:2

> And he said, Behold now, my lords, turn in, I pray you, into your servant's house, and tarry all night, and wash your feet, and ye shall rise up early, and go on your ways. And they said, Nay; but we will abide in the street all night.

---

81   . *Pentateuch & Haftorahs*, page 63.
82   . Broadman, volume 1, page 173.

Genesis 24:32

> And the man came into the house: and he ungirded his camels, and gave straw and provender for the camels, and water to wash his feet, and the men's feet that were with him.

Genesis 43:24

> And the man brought the men into Joseph's house, and gave them water, and they washed their feet; and he gave their asses provender.

Judges 19:21

> So he brought him into his house, and gave provender unto the asses: and they washed their feet, and did eat and drink.

1 Samuel 25:40–41

> 40. And when the servants of David were come to Abigail to Carmel, they spake unto her, saying, David sent us unto thee, to take thee to him to wife.
> 41. And she arose, and bowed herself on her face to the earth, and said, Behold, let thine handmaid be a servant to wash the feet of the servants of my lord.

The practice of washing one's feet might be the result of the earth (dust) as the dominion of Satan, and after walking the dusty roads, one's feet would be covered with dirt of the earth (sin).

Genesis 3:14–15

> 14. And the LORD God said unto the serpent, Because thou hast done this, thou art cursed above all cattle, and above every beast of the field; upon thy belly shalt thou go, and dust shalt thou eat all the days of thy life:
> 15. And I will put enmity between thee and the woman, and between thy seed and her seed; it shall bruise thy head, and thou shalt bruise his heel.

Christ Jesus crushes the Serpent's (Satan's) head, but the Serpent bites his heel. The dirt (the earth) is unclean because of death. As a result, sin affects the feet and must be washed away. This is a wonderful picture of what Christ Jesus did for a sinful world on Calvary's cross. As the water washes away the dirt of the road, the blood of Christ Jesus washes away the sin of our life, all that is required is to seek God's forgiveness.

Romans 10:13

> For whosoever shall call upon the name of the Lord shall be saved.

From the New Testament references of the ordinance of foot washing, Christ Jesus instituted foot washing:

John 13:5

> After that he poureth water into a bason, and began to wash the disciples' feet, and to wipe them with the towel wherewith he was girded.

Paul writing to Timothy about widows:

1 Timothy 5:10

> Well reported of for good works; if she have brought up children, if she have lodged strangers, if she have washed the saints' feet, if she have relieved the afflicted, if she have diligently followed every good work.

When the ordinance is practiced in the church the lessons taught are humility, equality, serving others, and as a symbol of sanctification as we come into contact with sin and temptation.

SARAH'S UNBELIEF REPROVED
Genesis 18:9–15

9. *And they said unto him, Where is Sarah thy wife? And he said, Behold, in the tent.*
10. *And he said, I will certainly return unto thee according to the time of life; and, lo, Sarah thy wife shall have a son. And Sarah heard it in the tent door, which was behind him.*
11. *Now Abraham and Sarah were old and well stricken in age; and it ceased to be with Sarah after the manner of women.*
12. *Therefore Sarah laughed within herself, saying, After I am waxed old shall I have pleasure, my Lord being old also?*
13. *And the LORD said unto Abraham, Wherefore did Sarah laugh, saying, Shall I of a surety bear a child, which am old?*

14. *Is any thing too hard for the LORD? At the time appointed I will return unto thee, according to the time of life, and Sarah shall have a son.*

15. *Then Sarah denied, saying, I laughed not; for she was afraid. And he said, Nay; but thou didst laugh.*

Sarah's disbelief is based on the fact that she and Abraham are very long in the tooth. She is close to fifty years past ovulation cycles, so she laughed. Some theologians have tried to say that Sarah was laughing with the joy of having a child of her own, but verse 13 clearly states laughter is the result of disbelief. Abraham laughed when God spoke to him saying he would have a son of his wife Sarah (Gen 17:17), but unlike Sarah, his was laughter of delight. Abraham was a man of faith; therefore, God said he and Sarah would have a son and that settled it—full stop.

Now God question, *Is anything too hard for the LORD?* The answer obviously is no. therefore, Sarah will get pregnant and deliver a son. Now Sarah knows that within the next year, she will truly be a mother.

Sarah laughs[83]

The Lord noted the honor she shows her husband by calling him lord in verse 13. Sarah is thus honored in scripture:

1 Peter 3:6
Even as Sara obeyed Abraham, calling him lord: whose daughters ye are, as long as ye do well, and are not afraid with any amazement.

Titus 2:5
To be discreet, chaste, keepers at home, good, obedient to their own husbands, that the word of God be not blasphemed.

83   . http://clipart.christiansunite.com/1320057661/Bible_Characters_Clipart/Abraham_Clipart/Abraham008.jpg.

GOD REVEALS THE DESTRUCTION OF SODOM
Genesis 18:16–22

16. *And the men rose up from thence, and looked toward Sodom: and Abraham went with them to bring them on the way.*

17. *And the LORD said, Shall I hide from Abraham that thing which I do;*

18. *Seeing that Abraham shall surely become a great and mighty nation, and all the nations of the earth shall be blessed in him?*

19. *For I know him, that he will command his children and his household after him, and they shall keep the way of the LORD, to do justice and judgment; that the LORD may bring upon Abraham that which he hath spoken of him.*

20. *And the LORD said, Because the cry of Sodom and Gomorrah is great, and because their sin is very grievous;*

21. *I will go down now, and see whether they have done altogether according to the cry of it, which is come unto me; and if not, I will know.*

22. *And the men turned their faces from thence, and went toward Sodom: but Abraham stood yet before the LORD.*

The two who are supposed to have been created angels went toward Sodom. The one who is called Jehovah throughout the chapter continued with Abraham and would not hide from him the thing he intended to do. Though God long forbears with sinners, from which they fancy that the Lord does not see and does not regard, yet when the day of his wrath comes, he will look toward them. The Lord will give Abraham an opportunity to intercede with him and show him the reason of his conduct. Consider, as a very bright part of Abraham's character and example that he not only prayed with his family, but he was very careful to teach and rule them well. Those who expect family blessings must make conscience of family duty. Abraham did not fill their heads with matters of doubtful dispute; but he taught them to be serious and devout in the worship of God, and to be honest in their dealings with all men. Of how few may such a character be given in our days! How little care is taken by masters of families to ground those under them in the principles of religion! Do we watch from sabbath to sabbath whether they go forward or backward?[84]

---

84   . Matthew Henry, volume 1, page 94.

ABRAHAM'S INTERCESSION FOR SODOM
Genesis 18:23–33

23. *And Abraham drew near, and said, Wilt thou also destroy the righteous with the wicked?*

24. *Peradventure there be fifty righteous within the city: wilt thou also destroy and not spare the place for the fifty righteous that are therein?*

25. *That be far from thee to do after this manner, to slay the righteous with the wicked: and that the righteous should be as the wicked, that be far from thee: Shall not the Judge of all the earth do right?*

26. *And the LORD said, If I find in Sodom fifty righteous within the city, then I will spare all the place for their sakes.*

27. *And Abraham answered and said, Behold now, I have taken upon me to speak unto the LORD, which am but dust and ashes:*

28. *Peradventure there shall lack five of the fifty righteous: wilt thou destroy all the city for lack of five? And he said, If I find there forty and five, I will not destroy it.*

29. *And he spake unto him yet again, and said, Peradventure there shall be forty found there. And he said, I will not do it for forty's sake.*

30. *And he said unto him, Oh let not the LORD be angry, and I will speak: Peradventure there shall thirty be found there. And he said, I will not do it, if I find thirty there.*

31. *And he said, Behold now, I have taken upon me to speak unto the LORD: Peradventure there shall be twenty found there. And he said, I will not destroy it for twenty's sake.*

32. *And he said, Oh let not the LORD be angry, and I will speak yet but this once: Peradventure ten shall be found there. And he said, I will not destroy it for ten's sake.*

33. *And the LORD went his way, as soon as he had left communing with Abraham: and Abraham returned unto his place.*

Here is the first solemn prayer upon record in the Bible; and it is a prayer for the sparing of Sodom. Abraham prayed earnestly that Sodom might be spared, if but a few righteous persons should be found in it. Come and learn from Abraham what compassion we should feel for sinners, and how earnestly we should pray for them. We see here that the prays of the righteous do avail much.

James 5:16

> Confess your faults one to another, and pray one for another, that ye may be healed. The effectual fervent prayer of a righteous man availeth much.

Abraham, indeed, failed in his request for the whole place, but Lot was miraculously delivered. Be encouraged then to expect, by earnest prayer, the blessing of God upon your families, your friends, your neighborhood. To this end, you must not only pray, but you must live like Abraham. He knew the Judge of all the earth would do right. He does not plead that the wicked may be spared for their own sake, or because it would be severe to destroy them, but for the sake of the righteous who might be found among them. And righteousness only can be made a plea before God. How then did Christ make intercession for transgressors? Not by blaming the Divine law, nor by alleging aught in extenuation or excuse of human guilt; but by pleading HIS OWN obedience unto death.[85]

---

85   Matthew Henry, volume 1, page 95

SODOM'S REWARD FOR DEBAUCHERY

Genesis 19

Lot Fleeing Sodom[86]

CHAPTER OVERVIEW

This chapter is a continuation of the Last. Chapter 18 ends with God agreeing not to destroy the city of Sodom for the sake of ten righteous people. The chapter opens with the arrival of the angels at the gates of Sodom. Lot, the nephew of Abraham, was sitting at the gates of the city and rose to greet them and entertain them for the night. However, the wickedness of the men of Sodom brought about the wrath of God. The angels removed Lot and his family from the city, and they fled to the city of Zoar. Once they were out of Sodom, God did destroy the city; Lot's wife's disobedience was also

---

86 . http://freechristimages.org/Images_Genesis/Lot_Fleeing_Sodom_BenjaminWest_1810.jpg,

dealt with. Lot with his daughters then fled to the mountains and lived in a cave, and while there, the daughters conceived and bore Lot grandsons/sons.

CHAPTER STRUCTURE

- The Goodness of Lot (1–3)
- The wickedness of the Sodomites (4–11)
- The securing of Lot and his family (12–23)
- God's wrath unleashed upon the cities of the plain (24–25)
- God's punishment for disobedience (26)
- The conflagration observed by Abraham (27–29)
- Incest and the descendants of Lot (30–38)

THE GOODNESS OF LOT
Genesis 19:1–3

1. *And there came two angels to Sodom at even; and Lot sat in the gate of Sodom: and Lot seeing them rose up to meet them; and he bowed himself with his face toward the ground;*
2. *And he said, Behold now, my lords, turn in, I pray you, into your servant's house, and tarry all night, and wash your feet, and ye shall rise up early, and go on your ways. And they said, Nay; but we will abide in the street all night.*
3. *And he pressed upon them greatly; and they turned in unto him, and entered into his house; and he made them a feast, and did bake unleavened bread, and they did eat.*

The two angels approached the gates of Sodom. Lot, sitting at the gate, rose to meet them, and as it was toward dark, Lot extended the hospitality of his home to the two strangers. It is obvious he saw them as normal human being, as of the use and spell of *"my lords,"* the lowercase indicates them as mortal. The two initially refused, but Lot insisted and they relented and Lot prepared them a feast.

The fact that Lot was sitting at the gate indicates he was a man of authority in the city of Sodom. The book of Job speaks of the city elders sitting at the gates:

Job 29:7–12
7. "When I went out to the gate by the city, When I took my seat in the open square,
8. The young men saw me and hid, And the aged arose *and* stood;
9. The princes refrained from talking, And put *their* hand on their mouth;
10. The voice of nobles was hushed, And their tongue stuck to the roof of their mouth.
11. When the ear heard, then it blessed me, And when the eye saw, then it approved me
12. Because I delivered the poor who cried out, The fatherless and *the one who* had no helper.

Lot could have gained dominance and eminence in as much as he had arrived with great substance:

Genesis 13:6
And the land was not able to bear them, that they might dwell together: for their substance was great, so that they could not dwell together.

Further, it is obvious he had obtained a house within the city upon arrival to the city of Sodom; after all, to be a city elder, one must reside in the city:

Genesis 13:12
Abram dwelled in the land of Canaan, and Lot dwelled in the cities of the plain, and pitched his tent toward Sodom.

It is more probable that he is riding on the coattails of his uncle Abraham. Shortly after Lot's move to Sodom, the city was overrun and plundered; Lot and other Sodom citizens were carried off. Upon hearing of this, Abram fielded a small army and, applying heroic skill and effort, freed the captives and returning the booty (Genesis 14:1–16). Lot's influence and prominence therefore is the result of being Abraham's nephew.

Is this the confirmation of Lot's righteousness that the apostle Peter wrote about in his epistle, Lot's generous hospitality, or was it he knew the depravity of the people of Sodom and if they spend the night in the streets they would not survive?

2 Peter 2:6–8

6. And turning the cities of Sodom and Gomorrha into ashes condemned them with an overthrow, making them an example unto those that after should live ungodly;

7. And delivered just Lot, vexed with the filthy conversation of the wicked:

8. (For that righteous man dwelling among them, in seeing and hearing, vexed his righteous soul from day to day with their unlawful deeds;)

THE WICKEDNESS OF THE SODOMITES
Genesis 19:4–11

4. *But before they lay down, the men of the city, even the men of Sodom, compassed the house round, both old and young, all the people from every quarter:*

5. *And they called unto Lot, and said unto him, Where are the men which came in to thee this night? bring them out unto us, that we may know them.*

6. *And Lot went out at the door unto them, and shut the door after him,*

7. *And said, I pray you, brethren, do not so wickedly.*

8. *Behold now, I have two daughters which have not known man; let me, I pray you, bring them out unto you, and do ye to them as is good in your eyes: only unto these men do nothing; for therefore came they under the shadow of my roof.*

9. *And they said, Stand back. And they said again, This one fellow came in to sojourn, and he will needs be a judge: now will we deal worse with thee, than with them. And they pressed sore upon the man, even Lot, and came near to break the door.*

10. *But the men put forth their hand, and pulled Lot into the house to them, and shut to the door.*

11. *And they smote the men that were at the door of the house with blindness, both small and great: so that they wearied themselves to find the door.*

Having dined and now relaxing in conversation or investigation as to the character and nature of the inhabitants of Sodom, the angels, to be true to God's agreement with Abraham, were attempting to ascertain if there were ten righteous people within the city:

Genesis 18:32
> And he said, Oh let not the LORD be angry, and I will speak yet but this once: Peradventure ten shall be found there. And he said, I will not destroy it for ten's sake

However, the citizens answer for Lot, laying siege to the house of Lot; the males of the city of every age from one end of the city to the other, and showing the general corruption and depravity of the city, that it was so far from having ten righteous inhabitants. Some were past committing the sin they were so infamous for, as well as those that burned with that unnatural lust; some that could not be actors were willing to be spectators; and all were curious to see the lovely persons that it was reported all over the city were seen to go into Lot's house.[87]

What Paul says also refers to the same point: that God punished the impiety of men, when he cast them into such a state of blindness, that they gave themselves up to abominable lusts, and dishonored their own bodies.[88]

Romans 1:18
> For the wrath of God is revealed from heaven against all ungodliness and unrighteousness of men, who hold the truth in unrighteousness;

Having surrounded the house, they now cry for Lot to turn them out that they may *know* them. Lot instead stepped and closed the door behind him. Obviously this was an attempt by Lot to protect his guest; within the Mideastern culture, these two men were under the protection of Lot.

It should be noted some rabbinical scholars argue that the sin was their being inhospitable to stranger. The Jewish Encyclopedia has information on the importance of hospitality to the Jewish people. The people of Sodom were seen as guilty of many other significant sins. Rabbinic writings affirm that the Sodomites also committed economic crimes, blasphemy, and bloodshed. One of the worst was to give money or even gold ingots to

---

87   . John Gill's commentary, http://www.ewordtoday.com/comments/.
88   . John Calvin, volume 1.

beggars, after inscribing their names on them, and then subsequently refusing to sell them food. The unfortunate stranger would end up starving, and after his death, the people who gave him the money would reclaim it. A rabbinic tradition, described in the Mishnah, postulates that the sin of Sodom was related to property: Sodomites believed that "what is mine is mine, and what is yours is yours" (Abot), which is interpreted as a lack of compassion. Another rabbinic tradition is that these two wealthy cities treated visitors in a sadistic fashion. One major crime done to strangers was almost identical to that of Procrustes in Greek mythology. This would be the story of the "bed" that guests to Sodom were forced to sleep in: if they were too short, they were stretched to fit it, and if they were too tall, they were cut up (indeed, in Hebrew and Yiddish, the corresponding term for a Procrustean bed is a "Sodom bed").[89]

However, this viewpoint is not supported by scripture. As lawful copulation with a man's wife is modestly expressed by knowing her:

Genesis 4:1
> And Adam *knew* Eve his wife; and she conceived, and bare Cain, and said, I have gotten a man from the LORD.

This unlawful and shocking copulation of man with man is expressed by this phrase; and that this was their meaning is plain from Lot's answer to them in verse 8. In offering his daughters to this degenerate mob let one to the conclusion that Lot knew these two men are the messengers of God. On the other hand, if he did not know them as angels but mortal men, he had lived so long in Sodom that he too was corrupted by the sin of the city residents. He would have his daughter gang-raped to protect two strangers, honoring the cultural rules, but dishonoring the laws of God.

The men of Sodom did not want the daughters, and they pressed Lot to surrender them and get out of the way or they would deal with him far harsher. At this point in the narrative, the two angels have had enough and took hold of Lot pulling into the house and shut the door. They then blinded them *"so that they wearied themselves to find the door."* The word for "blindness" is only used here and denotes a peculiar sort of blindness; not an entire blindness with respect to every object, but only with regard to that they were intent upon; for otherwise they would not have continued about Lot's house, or fatigued themselves with searching for the door of it, but would

---

89   . JewishEncyclopedia.com, The unedited full text of the 1906 Jewish Encyclopedia.

rather have been glad to have groped to their own houses as well as they could, and so these men of Sodom could see other objects, but not the door of Lot's house. Their heads were so confused, and their imaginations so disturbed as if drunken men; or the medium of the visual faculty, so altered the form of the object to be seen so changed, that they could not discern it. When they saw the door, it looked like the wall, and that which seemed to them to be the door proved to be the wall: so that they wearied themselves to find the door; went backward and forward, fancying the door was here, and then it was there, and when they came to it, they perceived it was not; and thus they went to and fro, until they were quite weary of seeking it, and despaired of finding it, and left off.[90]

THE SECURING OF LOT AND HIS FAMILY
Genesis 19:12–23

12. *And the men said unto Lot, Hast thou here any besides? son in law, and thy sons, and thy daughters, and whatsoever thou hast in the city, bring them out of this place:*

13. *For we will destroy this place, because the cry of them is waxen great before the face of the LORD; and the LORD hath sent us to destroy it.*

14. *And Lot went out, and spake unto his sons in law, which married his daughters, and said, Up, get you out of this place; for the LORD will destroy this city. But he seemed as one that mocked unto his sons in law.*

15. *And when the morning arose, then the angels hastened Lot, saying, Arise, take thy wife, and thy two daughters, which are here; lest thou be consumed in the iniquity of the city.*

16. *And while he lingered, the men laid hold upon his hand, and upon the hand of his wife, and upon the hand of his two daughters; the LORD being merciful unto him: and they brought him forth, and set him without the city.*

17. *And it came to pass, when they had brought them forth abroad, that he said, Escape for thy life; look not behind thee, neither stay thou in all the plain; escape to the mountain, lest thou be consumed.*

18. *And Lot said unto them, Oh, not so, my LORD:*

19. *Behold now, thy servant hath found grace in thy sight, and thou hast magnified thy mercy, which thou hast shewed unto me in saving my life; and I cannot escape to the mountain, lest some evil take me, and I die:*

---

90   . John Gill's commentary, http://www.ewordtoday.com/comments.

20. Behold now, this city is near to flee unto, and it is a little one: Oh, let me escape thither, (is it not a little one?) and my soul shall live.

21. And he said unto him, See, I have accepted thee concerning this thing also, that I will not overthrow this city, for the which thou hast spoken.

22. Haste thee, escape thither; for I cannot do anything till thou be come thither. Therefore the name of the city was called Zoar.

23. The sun was risen upon the earth when Lot entered into Zoar.

The angels revealed themselves to Lot and told him to get his family out: sons, sons-in-law, daughters, and whatever he had in the city to bring it out for God is going to destroy the whole of the cities of the plain.

Lot did just that. However, his sons-in-law thought he was making sport of them and did nothing. This is a sad commentary, because Lot obviously had not made effort to share his faith. For had he done so, they would not have looked upon his words and actions as just, but would have acted on his words.

Is this not what we are to do, share our faith and win the lost for Christ Jesus? The day is coming (and soon) when it will be too late, and we do not want our loved one left behind!

Morning arose and the messenger of God commanded Lot to take his wife and daughter and get out of the city now. He lingered, one can only speculate as to reason for their delay, but one could the think the world was appealing and they did not want to give it up. Therefore, the messenger lay holt of them and put them out of the city.

Note:

The wording of verse 16 makes one think they teleported then out of the city. The phrase "*they brought him forth, and set him without the city*" indicates something other than to walk.

The angel told them to flee to the mountains, but Lot being a lover of the city begged to flee to the city of Zoar, which he was permitted to do. Further the angel stated not to look back but straight ahead. Once we accept the Lord Christ Jesus as the master of our life, we are not to look back. In other words, we are made anew and dwelling the past only brings on trouble, confusion, and we cannot reach maturity in the Lord. The past is filled with pain, suffering, and discontentment, and if the enemy can keep one in the past, our relationship with other and our Lord will be diminished. Therefore, look forward and allow God's Holy Spirit to be a guide for our life and His word a light onto our path in life.

GOD'S WRATH UNLEASHED UPON THE CITIES OF THE PLAIN
Genesis 19:24–25

24. *Then the LORD rained upon Sodom and upon Gomorrah brimstone and fire from the LORD out of heaven;*
25. *And he overthrew those cities, and all the plain, and all the inhabitants of the cities, and that which grew upon the ground.*

Once Lot and his family were safely away from the plain, God rained down fire and brimstone upon the cities of the plain, turned it into a sea of asphaltites, or the Dead Sea:

Deuteronomy 29:23

> And that the whole land thereof is brimstone, and salt, and burning, that it is not sown, nor beareth, nor any grass groweth therein, like the overthrow of Sodom, and Gomorrah, Admah, and Zeboim, which the LORD overthrew in his anger, and in his wrath.

GOD'S PUNISHMENT FOR DISOBEDIENCE
Genesis 19:26

26. *But his wife looked back from behind him, and she became a pillar of salt.*

As they were going from Sodom to Zoar, she was behind Lot, his back was to her, so that he could not see her; this was a temptation to her to look back, since her husband could not see her, and this she did, either as the above paraphrases suggest, that she might see what would be the end of her father's house and family, or whether her married daughters, if she had any, were following her, after whom her bowels yearned, or being grieved for the goods and substance left behind, and for the people of Sodom in general, for whom she had too much concern. However, be it on what account it may, she was severely punished for it.[91]

Note:

> Rabbinical scholars have written her name as Adith or Irith, and according to the Targum of Jonathan, she was a native of Sodom.

She became a pillar of salt; her body was at once changed into a metallic substance, a kind of salt, hard and durable. That she did not fall to the ground, but stood up erect as a pillar, retaining very probably the human form, Josephus[92] says, this pillar continued to his times, and that he saw it.

THE CONFLAGRATION OBSERVED BY ABRAHAM
Genesis 19:27–29

27. *And Abraham gat up early in the morning to the place where he stood before the LORD:*
28. *And he looked toward Sodom and Gomorrah, and toward all the land of the plain, and beheld, and, lo, the smoke of the country went up as the smoke of a furnace.*
29. *And it came to pass, when God destroyed the cities of the plain, that God remembered Abraham, and sent Lot out of the midst of the overthrow, when he overthrew the cities in the which Lot dwelt.*

Our God cannot look upon sin, and as He brought judgment upon the cities of the plain for their abominable act, so too he will have Babylon destroyed:

Revelation 19:
2. For true and righteous are his judgments: for he hath judged the great whore, which did corrupt the earth with her fornication, and hath avenged the blood of his servants at her hand.
3. And again they said, Alleluia And her smoke rose up for ever and ever.

---

91   . John Gill's commentary, http://www.ewordtoday.com/comments.
92   . Josephus, Antiquities of the Jews, volume 1.

Abraham arose early, probability is that it is the morning following His visitation, to see if there where ten righteous people, and seeing devastation, he knew their sinfulness was complete.

INCEST AND THE DESCENDANTS OF LOT
Genesis 19:30–38

30. *And Lot went up out of Zoar, and dwelt in the mountain, and his two daughters with him; for he feared to dwell in Zoar: and he dwelt in a cave, he and his two daughters.*

31. *And the firstborn said unto the younger, Our father is old, and there is not a man in the earth to come in unto us after the manner of all the earth:*

32. *Come, let us make our father drink wine, and we will lie with him, that we may preserve seed of our father.*

33. *And they made their father drink wine that night: and the firstborn went in, and lay with her father; and he perceived not when she lay down, nor when she arose.*

34. *And it came to pass on the morrow, that the firstborn said unto the younger, Behold, I lay yesternight with my father: let us make him drink wine this night also; and go thou in, and lie with him, that we may preserve seed of our father.*

35. *And they made their father drink wine that night also: and the younger arose, and lay with him; and he perceived not when she lay down, nor when she arose.*

36. *Thus were both the daughters of Lot with child by their father.*

37. *And the first born bare a son, and called his name Moab: the same is the father of the Moabites unto this day.*

38. *And the younger, she also bare a son, and called his name Benammi: the same is the father of the children of Ammon unto this day.*

LOT AND HIS DAUGHTERS[93]

Lot finally followed the words of the messenger and flew to the mountains and lived in a cave. His departure from Zoar was most likely brought on by the fact that inhabitants were as wicked as those of the other cities and were unreformed by the judgment on them. So he might fear that a like shower of fire would descend on them and destroy them, as it had the rest, though it had been spared for a while at his intercession; and according to the Jewish writers, it remained but one year after Sodom.[94]

Josephus makes mention of the mountains of Engedi; and here was a cave, where David with six hundred men were, in the sides of it, when Saul went into it; and perhaps may be the same cave where Lot and his two daughters lived.

1 Samuel 24:1

> And it came to pass, when Saul was returned from following the Philistines, that it was told him, saying, Behold, David is in the wilderness of Engedi.

---

93   . Hendrick Goltzius. 1558–1617, *Lot and his daughters*. 1616. Oil on canvas. 140 × 204 cm (55.1 × 80.3 in). Amsterdam, Rijksmuseum Amsterdam. Shows Lot being seduced by his two daughters. The fox behind the tree symbolizes female cunning. In the background in front of the burning city is the pillar of salt, Lot's wife. http://en.wikipedia.org/wiki/File:Lot_and_his_Daughters.jpg.

94   . John Gill's commentary, http://www.ewordtoday.com/comments.

His daughters conspired to commit a monstrously vile act. Now the daughter on two consecutive night got their father inebriated with wine, the most likely source of this was Zoar, to the point he was blind drunk, and not cognizant of his actions. First the elder then the younger and both did conceive and bring fore a male child.

One might ask the question of why would they think there are no other people on the earth; after all, there is Uncle Abraham. But of course, they may never have traveled to visit with him and could be completely unaware. Therefore, after seeing the destruction of the cities of the plain, their thinking is "we's it." We are the remnant of humanity; from verse 31, *there is not a man in the earth to come in unto us after the manner of all the earth.*

The firstborn born a son and named him Moab, which means from the father. Obviously she was not ashamed of her sexual impurity. Out of vile act come the Moabites, which Ruth is a descendant and from her steamed our Lord and savior:

Matthew 1:5
And Salmon begat Booz of Rachab; and Booz begat Obed of Ruth; and Obed begat Jesse

The younger sister born a son and named him Benammi, which means "the son of my people," and he is the father of the Ammonites. The two are called the children of Lot:

Psalm 83:8
Assur also is joined with them: they have holpen the children of Lot. Selah.

And he is honored in:

2 Peter 2:7
And delivered just Lot, vexed with the filthy conversation of the wicked.

DECEITFUL ABRAHAM
Genesis 20

God Came to Abimelech in a Dream[95]

CHAPTER OVERVIEW

Once again in this chapter, Abraham reveals his weakness when it comes to trusting God's word. Just as he denied his relationship with Sarah as his wife, to Pharaoh in chapter 12, he does so again. Abraham journeyed to the city and area of Gerar and settled in that area. God rebukes the king of Gerar in a dream, and he expresses his revulsion at the way Abraham had used him. The king then restores Sarah to Abraham.

---

95   . http://jacobisrael71.files.wordpress.com/2011/09/healing-blind-man-300x300.jpg.

Abraham then prays for the king and his house and they are healing. The scripture is impartial in relating the blemishes even of its most celebrated patriarch.

CHAPTER STRUCTURE

- Abraham Sojourned to Gerar (1)
- Abraham's Sin in Denying His Wife (2)
- God's Discourse with Abimelech (3)
- God Accepts Abimelech's Plea (4–6)
- God Directs Abimelech to Make Restitution (7)
- Abimelech's Discourse of Disgust with Abraham (8–10)
- Abraham's Reply of Explanation (11–13)
- Abimelech Restores Sarah to Abraham (14–16)
- Abraham Prays for God to Remove His Judgment (17–18)

ABRAHAM SOJOURNED TO GERAR
Genesis 20:1

1. *And Abraham journeyed from thence toward the south country, and dwelled between Kadesh and Shur, and sojourned in Gerar.*

So Abraham moves to Gerar and we are not told the reason for the relocation. After living in the region of Mamre for about twenty years, he now moves into the land controlled by the Philistines. There are several possibilities for his moving: (1) after the destruction of the cities of the plain and their surrounding areas, the pastures is no longer good for grazing animals. (2) Terrified by the magnitude of the desolation of God's mighty hand, Abraham flees to safety. (3) As the rabbinical scholars have written, Abraham was grieved by the incestuous acts committed by Lot and his daughters. (4) The reproach of the Canaanites cast on him and his faith in the one and only God because of his extended family.[96] (5) Abraham was so deeply affected with the melancholy prospect of the ruined cities, and not knowing what was become of his nephew Lot and his family, that he could no longer bear to dwell within sight of the place.

---

96   . Matthew Henry, volume 1, page.

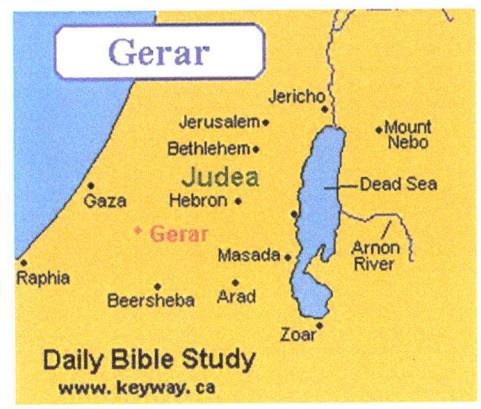

Map of Gerar Location

Gerar, or Gerara: known as Tell Abu Hurayrah by archaeologist. Gerar, meaning "lodging place," was a Philistine town and district in what is today south central Israel. Archaeological evidence points to the town having come into existence with the arrival of the Philistines at around 1200 BC and having been little more than a village until 800–700 BC.[97]

Gerar was an ancient town in the Negev, in the south of the land of Israel, roughly halfway between Beersheba and Gaza.[98]

ABRAHAM'S SIN IN DENYING HIS WIFE
Genesis 20:2

2. *And Abraham said of Sarah his wife, She is my sister: and Abimelech king of Gerar sent, and took Sarah.*

Once again, Abraham has a lapse of faith in that he had his wife Sarah as his sister; when God said he would be the father of multitudes. The same as he said to Pharaoh:

Genesis 12:7–9

7. Say, I pray thee, thou art my sister: that it may be well with me for thy sake; and my soul shall live because of thee.

8. And it came to pass, that, when Abram was come into Egypt, the Egyptians beheld the woman that she was very fair.

9. The princes also of Pharaoh saw her, and commended her before Pharaoh: and the woman was taken into Pharaoh's house.

His sin of unbelief and deception is worse than that of Egypt, for Sarah is mother of the heir of promise, and could be pregnant with Isaac. Abraham, patriarch of the Hebrews, would prostitute his wife for his security.

---

97 . http://www.christusrex.org/www1/ofm/mad/legends/legends107.html.
98 . http://www.keyway.ca/htm2001/20010115.htm.

Now Sarah was ninety years old at this point, so why would Abimelech take Sarah into his harem? There are possibilities: (1) it might be that God had regenerated her to that of a child-bearing woman, not only the inward parts, but her outward appearance. (2) Sarah was a very beautiful woman, and she has not had children; therefore, she may have aged gently, and appear younger than her years. (3) More than likely, Abimelech took Sarah to form an alliance with Abraham, who was very rich, and of his successful accomplishments. A petty king, such as Abimelech, would naturally be glad to form an alliance with such a powerful chief as Abraham was; we cannot but recollect his late defeat of the four confederate Canaanite kings.[99]

GOD'S DISCOURSE WITH ABIMELECH
Genesis 20:3

3. But God came to Abimelech in a dream by night, and said to him, Behold, thou art but a dead man, for the woman which thou hast taken; for she is a man's wife.

God appeared to Abimelech in a dream to prevent him from sinning and to preserve the purity of Sarah. We may be despised by the world we are yet precious to him, since for our sake he reproves even kings, as it is written:

Psalm 105:14
> He suffered no man to do them wrong: yea, he reproved kings for their sakes.

In this verse, God tell Abimelech that because he has taken this woman, Sarah a married woman, without her consent, or ascertaining the relationship and connection with Abraham, he is a dead man.[100] This verse should serve as a warning to all of mankind just how God's view of adultery is to be avenged by Him, and from God's Word, we find the following:

Leviticus 20:10
> And the man that committeth adultery with another man's wife, even he that committeth adultery with his neighbour's wife, the adulterer and the adulteress shall surely be put to death.

---

99   . http://www.godrules.net/library/clarke/clarkegen20.htm.
100   . John Gill's Exposition of the Entire Bible, ttp://www.ewordtoday.com/comments/genesis/gill/genesis20.htm.

God requires mutual fidelity be cherished between husbands and wives, and they are to consider their marriage sacred. God then presides over marriage and will take vengeance on those who defile the marriage bed.[101]

Hebrews 13:4

> Marriage is honourable in all, and the bed undefiled: but whoremongers and adulterers God will judge.

GOD ACCEPTS ABIMELECH'S PLEA
Genesis 20:4–6

4. *But Abimelech had not come near her: and he said, LORD, wilt thou slay also a righteous nation?*
5. *Said he not unto me, She is my sister? and she, even she herself said, He is my brother: in the integrity of my heart and innocency of my hands have I done this.*
6. *And God said unto him in a dream, Yea, I know that thou didst this in the integrity of thy heart; for I also withheld thee from sinning against me: therefore suffered I thee not to touch her.*

Not only did come to Abimelech, but he addressed God as Adonai, a term used by the Hebrews when addressing God the Father. There is a definite similarity between Abimelech and Melchizedek, for the Hebrew word for king appears in both names. It would appear that this non-Hebrew monarch worshipped the God of Abraham.[102]

The phrase, *wilt thou slay also a righteous nation,* may be a reference to the destruction of the cities of the plain for they were cities of sin. The more likely is that as king, if condemned, then the whole nation is condemned; after all, the king represents the people, just as the president represents the people of the United States. Therefore, he pleas his ignorance that Abraham and Sarah are married, that he only acted on the facts as stated by them, he is innocent![103] He further states he took her to wife with honest motives. For it is written in scriptures:

---

101 . John Calvin Commentary, volume 1, page.
102 . The Broadman Bible Commentary, volume 1, page 181.
103 . Matthew Henry, volume 1, page 103.

1 John 3:21

> Beloved, if our heart condemn us not, then have we confidence toward God.

Abraham was practicing situational ethics, not trusting in the sovereign power of a living, and loving God. After the great victory in chapter 14, God had told him earlier, "I am thy shield":[104]

Genesis 15:1

> After these things the word of the LORD came unto Abram in a vision, saying, Fear not, Abram: I am thy shield, and thy exceeding great reward.

In verse 6, God acknowledged Abimelech's innocence; however, God does chastise him, for by human judgment, you are not guilty, but in God's eye, no one is without sin.

Romans 3:23

> For all have sinned, and come short of the glory of God.

I also withheld thee from sinning against me: John Calvin makes this observation about this phrase:[105]

> This declaration implies that God had respect, not only to Abraham, but also to the king. For because he had no intention of defiling another man's wife, God had compassion on him. And it frequently happens, that the Spirit restrains, by his bridle, those who are gliding into error; just as, on the other hand, he drives those headlong, by infatuation, and a spirit of stupor, who, with depraved affection and lust, knowingly transgress… so He proves Himself daily to be the faithful guardian of his own people, to prevent them from rushing forward, from lighter faults to desperate crimes.

It is great mercy to hinder from committing sin; of this God must have the glory, whoever is the instrument. As an example from scriptures, David being stopped by Abigail:

---

104   . The Parallel Bible Commentary, page 57.
105   . Calvin Commentaries, volume 1, page 525.

1 Samuel 25:32–33

> 32. And David said to Abigail, Blessed be the LORD God of Israel, which sent thee this day to meet me:
>
> 33. And blessed be thy advice, and blessed be thou, which hast kept me this day from coming to shed blood, and from avenging myself with mine own hand.

GOD DIRECTS ABIMELECH TO MAKE RESTITUTION
Genesis 20:7

> 7. *Now therefore restore the man his wife; for he is a prophet, and he shall pray for thee, and thou shalt live: and if thou restore her not, know thou that thou shalt surely die, thou, and all that are thine.*

God tells Abimelech that Abraham is a prophet and his intercessory prayer would remove the guilt and lead to salvation. A prophet: the God-addressed inspiration constitutes the essence of prophecy. Abraham was the recipient of divine revelation, and was thereby placed in so confidential a relation to God, that he could intercede for sinners, and atone for sins of infirmity through his intercession.[106]

This is the first reference to a prophet in the Bible. Usually the prophets were preaching a message that God had instructed them to warm the Israelites to repent of their sin and return unto God. Abraham as intercessor is one of the most important functions of the early prophets:[107]

Deuteronomy 9:20

> And the LORD was very angry with Aaron to have destroyed him: and I prayed for Aaron also the same time.

1 Samuel 7:5

> And Samuel said, Gather all Israel to Mizpeh, and I will pray for you unto the LORD.

---

106   . Keil & Delitzsch Commentary on the Old Testament, volume 1, page 153.
107   . The Broadman Bible Commentary, volume 1, page 181.

1 Samuel 12:19, 23

> 19. And all the people said unto Samuel, Pray for thy servants unto the LORD thy God, that we die not: for we have added unto all our sins this evil, to ask us a king.
>
> 23. Moreover as for me, God forbid that I should sin against the LORD in ceasing to pray for you: but I will teach you the good and the right way.

Jeremiah 7:16

> Therefore pray not thou for this people, neither lift up cry nor prayer for them, neither make intercession to me: for I will not hear thee.

Jeremiah 27:18

> But if they be prophets, and if the word of the LORD be with them, let them now make intercession to the LORD of hosts, that the vessels which are left in the house of the LORD, and in the house of the king of Judah, and at Jerusalem, go not to Babylon.

From this verse, one should ascertain how God the Father sees the believer; if a person is a born-again believer in the Lord Christ Jesus, then God sees the blood of Christ covering all the blemishes. Even so, one that stumbles must seek the Lord's forgiveness. Sin has an ending, death. We all face death, which is the result of sin. The physical death is the result of Adam and Eve sinning in the Garden of Eden. But a far worse death is the spiritual death:

Revelation 21:8

> But the fearful, and unbelieving, and the abominable, and murderers, and whoremongers, and sorcerers, and idolaters, and all liars, shall have their part in the lake which burneth with fire and brimstone: which is the second death.

ABIMELECH'S DISCOURSE OF DISGUST WITH ABRAHAM
Genesis 20:8–10

> 8. *Therefore Abimelech rose early in the morning, and called all his servants, and told all these things in their ears: and the men were sore afraid.*

9. *Then Abimelech called Abraham, and said unto him, What hast thou done unto us? and what have I offended thee, that thou hast brought on me and on my kingdom a great sin? thou hast done deeds unto me that ought not to be done.*

10. *And Abimelech said unto Abraham, What sawest thou, that thou hast done this thing?*

Upon the king awaking, he calls his adviser and counselor telling them of the visitation of the Almighty and their conversation. They were fearful, because they understood what God had told Abimelech in verse 7 also is applicable to them.

It is interesting to note, Abimelech does not cast all the burden of this sin onto Abraham, but retained a share of the guilt by the phrase *"what have I offended thee."* Unlike the hypocrites are in the habit of doing; the moment they can accuse others, they then absolve themselves of any sinfulness. It is however to be noted that adultery is here called a great sin, because it binds not one man only, but a whole people, as in a common crime. The king of Gerar could not indeed have spoken thus had he not acknowledged the sacred right of marriage.[108] Unlike so many of today's so-called Christians characterized by the jesting of their adulteress relationships. For the disobedient bring down the wrath of God:

1 Corinthians 5:10
> Yet not altogether with the fornicators of this world, or with the covetous, or extortioners, or with idolaters; for then must ye needs go out of the world.

Ephesians 5:6
> Let no man deceive you with vain words: for because of these things cometh the wrath of God upon the children of disobedience.

What sawest thou, that thou hast done this thing? By this statement, the king wants to know what Abraham saw that he would stoop to such deception. Were the people or king so lustful that they would stop at nothing to satisfy their lust, causing Abraham to feel his life would be in jeopardy?[109]

---

108   . Calvin Commentaries, volume 1, page 525.
109   . John Gill's Exposition of the Entire Bible, http://www.ewordtoday.com/comments/genesis/gill/genesis20.htm.

ABRAHAM'S REPLY OF EXPLANATION
Genesis 20:11–13

11. And Abraham said, Because I thought, Surely the fear of God is not in this place; and they will slay me for my wife's sake.

12. And yet indeed she is my sister; she is the daughter of my father, but not the daughter of my mother; and she became my wife.

13. And it came to pass, when God caused me to wander from my father's house, that I said unto her, This is thy kindness which thou shalt shew unto me; at every place whither we shall come, say of me, He is my brother.

Abraham pleads a poor excuse. Not have been in this region before, Abraham thought the worst. For little is expected where God is not revered:

Psalms 36:1
>   The transgression of the wicked saith within my heart, that there is no fear of God before his eyes.

There are places and people that have a reverence for God, although they don't follow the edicts we associate with Christian. These differences could simply be cultural or regional; therefore, we conclude they have no fear of God. This does an injustice to both Christ Jesus and Christian, and makes us obnoxious to God's judgment:

Matthew 7:1
>   Judge not, that ye be not judged.

Uncharitable and censoriousness are sins that are the cause of many other sins. When men have once persuaded themselves concerning such and such that they have not the fear of God, they think this will justify them in the most unjust and unchristian practices toward them. Men would not do ill if they did not first think ill.[110]

Abraham's excuse for the lie "she is my sister" as only Sarah is his half sister, but those to whom he said, *She is my sister,* understood that she was so his sister as not to be capable of being his wife, so that it was an equivocation, with an intent to deceive.

---

110   . Matthew Henry, volume 1, page 105.

He clears himself from the imputation of an affront designed to Abimelech in it by alleging that it had been his practice before, according to an agreement between him and his wife, when they first became sojourners.[111] A poor defense Abraham made. The statement absolved him from the charge of direct and absolute falsehood, but he had told a moral untruth because there was an intention to deceive (compare Genesis 12:11–13). "Honesty is always the best policy." Abraham's life would have been as well protected without the fraud as with it: and what shame to himself, what distrust to God, what dishonor to religion might have been prevented! "Let us speak truth every man to his neighbor."[112]

Zechariah 8:16

> These are the things that ye shall do; Speak ye every man the truth to his neighbour; execute the judgment of truth and peace in your gates.

Ephesians 4:25

> Wherefore putting away lying, speak every man truth with his neighbour: for we are members one of another.

ABIMELECH RESTORES SARAH TO ABRAHAM
Genesis 20:14–16

14. *And Abimelech took sheep, and oxen, and menservants, and womenservants, and gave them unto Abraham, and restored him Sarah his wife.*
15. *And Abimelech said, Behold, my land is before thee: dwell where it pleaseth thee.*
16. *And unto Sarah he said, Behold, I have given thy brother a thousand pieces of silver: behold, he is to thee a covering of the eyes, unto all that are with thee, and with all other: thus she was reproved.*

And Abimelech took sheep, and oxen, and menservants, and womenservants, and gave them unto Abraham. In a good measure satisfied with what Abraham had said to excuse himself; and these gifts he gave unto him, that he might, as Jarchi observes, pray and intercede for him, that he and his family might be healed, having understood by the

---

111 . Matthew Henry, volume 1, page 105.
112 . Jamieson, Faussett, and Brown Bible Commentary; http://www.ewordtoday.com/comments/genesis/jfb/genesis20.htm.

divine oracle that he was a prophet, and if he prayed for him, he would be restored to health: and these were not given to bribe him to give his consent that Sarah might be continued with him, since it follows, and restored him Sarah his wife; untouched by him, as he was directed by God to do.[113]

And Abimelech said, behold, my whole land is before thee. Instead of bidding him be gone, and sending him away in haste out of his country, as the king of Egypt did in a like case, he solicits his stay in it; and to encourage him to it, makes an offer of his whole kingdom to him, to choose which part of it he would to dwell in: dwell where it pleaseth thee. If there was anyone part of it better than another, or more convenient for him, his family and his flocks, he was welcome to it.[114]

And unto Sarah he said, behold, I have given thy brother a thousand pieces of silver,

Some think that the sheep, oxen, etc., Abimelech had given to Abraham, were worth so many pieces of silver: but it rather seems that he gave these over and above them, and chiefly for Sarah's use, as will be observed hereafter; since the words are directed to her, and in which there is a sharp cutting expression, calling Abraham her brother, and not her husband, thereby putting her in mind and upbraiding her with her equivocation and dissimulation.

Abraham, being now known to be the husband of Sarah, would for the future be a covering to her, that no one should look upon her, and desire her, and take her to be his wife; and he would also be a protection to her maidens that were with her, the wives of his servants, that these also might not be taken from him: but it seems best to refer this to the gift of the thousand pieces of silver, and read the words, "behold, this is to thee a covering of the eyes"; so the Targums of Jonathan and Jerusalem; for the words are a continued biting sarcasm on Sarah; as Abimelech twits her with calling Abraham her brother in the preceding clause, so in this he tells her that he had given him so much money to buy her a veil with, and to supply her with veils from time to time to cover her eyes, that nobody might be tempted to lust after her, and that it might be known she was a married woman; for in these countries, married women wore veils for distinction:

---

113   . John Gill's Exposition of the Entire Bible, http://www.ewordtoday.com/comments/genesis/gill/genesis20.htm.
114   . John Gill's Exposition of the Entire Bible, http://www.ewordtoday.com/comments/genesis/gill/genesis20.htm.

Genesis 24:65

> For she had said unto the servant, What man is this that walketh in the field to meet us? And the servant had said, It is my master: therefore she took a vail, and covered herself.

And so not to be had by another, nor would any be deceived by her; and not only was this money given to buy veils for her, but for her female servants also that were married, that they might be known to be another's property; though this latter phrase "unto," or "with all that [are] with thee", may be understood, not of persons, but of things, even of all the girls which Abimelech had given her while in his house. These he did not take back again, but continued them with her, either for the above use, or whatever she pleased; and the following phrase, and with all this that Abimelech had said and done, thus she was reproved. Sarah was reproved for saying that Abraham was her brother: or the words may be rendered thus, "and so before all she was reproved"; before her husband, and before Abimelech's courtiers, and perhaps before her own servants; though Ainsworth, and others, take them to be the words of Abimelech, and render them, "and all that," or, "all this is that thou mayest be rebuked" or instructed. All that I have said and done is for this end, that thou mayest be warned and be careful for the future to speak out truth, without any equivocation, and not call Abraham thy brother, when he is thy husband.[115]

ABRAHAM PRAYS FOR GOD TO REMOVE HIS JUDGMENT
Genesis 20:17–18

> 17. *So Abraham prayed unto God: and God healed Abimelech, and his wife, and his maidservants; and they bare children.*
> 18. *For the LORD had fast closed up all the wombs of the house of Abimelech, because of Sarah Abraham's wife.*

The kindness of a prophet which Abraham showed to Abimelech: he *prayed for him,* v. 17, 18. This honors God would put upon Abraham that, though Abimelech had restored Sarah, the judgment he was under should be removed upon the prayer of Abraham, and not before. Thus God healed Miriam, when Moses, whom she had most affronted, prayed for her:

---

115   . John Gill's Exposition of the Entire Bible, http://www.ewordtoday.com/comments/genesis/gill/genesis20.htm.

Numbers 12:13

> And Moses cried unto the LORD, saying, Heal her now, O God, I beseech thee.

and was reconciled to Job's friends when Job, whom they had grieved, prayed for them:

Job 42:8–10

> 8. Therefore take unto you now seven bullocks and seven rams, and go to my servant Job, and offer up for yourselves a burnt offering; and my servant Job shall pray for you: for him will I accept: lest I deal with you after your folly, in that ye have not spoken of me the thing which is right, like my servant Job.
>
> 9. So Eliphaz the Temanite and Bildad the Shuhite and Zophar the Naamathite went, and did according as the LORD commanded them: the LORD also accepted Job.
>
> 10. And the LORD turned the captivity of Job, when he prayed for his friends: also the LORD gave Job twice as much as he had before.

And so did, as it were, give it under his hand that he was reconciled to them. Note, the prayers of good men may be a kindness to great men, and ought to be valued.[116]

James 5:16

> Confess your faults one to another, and pray one for another, that ye may be healed. The effectual fervent prayer of a righteous man availeth much.

This passage of has a negative side and that being: The fervent prayer of an unrighteous man and woman avail nothing. For instruction to become a righteous person, see pages 17 and 18.

---

116   . Matthew Henry, volume 1, page 106.

THE BIRTH OF THE SON OF PROMISE

Genesis 21

Laughter[117]

CHAPTER OVERVIEW

Following Abraham's admittance of deception and gaining forgiveness from both Abimelech and God, the omnipotent Almighty God, who prepared her that she would conceive and give birth to a son, visits Sarah. This joyous event is then followed by to some seems to be heartless on the part of Abraham—the expulsion of Hagar and her

---

117   . Laughter, by Mike Bennett (2011); http://biblicalgenealogy.kavonrueter.com/Pictur151.jpg.

son Ishmael. Abimelech seeks and gets a treaty with Abraham. Finally, Abraham gives praise and glory unto God, and the chapter closes by stating that Abraham resided in Philistine for some time.

CHAPTER STRUCTURE

- The birth of the promised son, Isaac (1–8)
- Expulsion of Hagar and Ishmael (9–21)
- Abraham and Abimelech make a treaty (22–32)
- Abraham worshiped God (33–34)

THE BIRTH OF THE PROMISED SON, ISAAC
Genesis 21:1–8

1. *And the LORD visited Sarah as he had said, and the LORD did unto Sarah as he had spoken.*
2. *For Sarah conceived, and bare Abraham a son in his old age, at the set time of which God had spoken to him.*
3. *And Abraham called the name of his son that was born unto him, whom Sarah bare to him, Isaac.*
4. *And Abraham circumcised his son Isaac being eight days old, as God had commanded him.*
5. *And Abraham was an hundred years old, when his son Isaac was born unto him.*
6. *And Sarah said, God hath made me to laugh, so that all that hear will laugh with me.*
7. *And she said, Who would have said unto Abraham, that Sarah should have given children suck? for I have born him a son in his old age.*
8. *And the child grew, and was weaned: and Abraham made a great feast the same day that Isaac was weaned.*

The Birth of Isaac
Verses 1 and 2

As one reads these verses, the reader will note the similarities between these and these passages:

Luke 1:31–36

31. And the angel said unto her, Fear not, Mary: for thou hast found favor with God.
32. And, behold, thou shalt conceive in thy womb, and bring forth a son, and shalt call his name JESUS.
33. He shall be great, and shall be called the Son of the Highest: and the Lord God shall give unto him the throne of his father David:
34. And he shall reign over the house of Jacob for ever; and of his kingdom there shall be no end.
35. Then said Mary unto the angel, How shall this be, seeing I know not a man?
36. And the angel answered and said unto her, The Holy Ghost shall come upon thee, and the power of the Highest shall overshadow thee: therefore also that holy thing which shall be born of thee shall be called the Son of God.

The circumstance of Isaac's conception and birth is a forerunner of the birth of Christ Jesus to show all of humanity that as God prepared Sarah: (1) the physical capacity to conceive and bear a child; (2) the mental and emotional ability to handle a child through all stages of development. So too he prepared Mary for the birth of Christ Jesus.[118]

As with Sarah, a womb that was dead, and with Mary who knew no man, God worked a miracle, which Isaac being the child of promises, he being one of the foundation stones from which sprang fore our Savior and Lord Christ Jesus. In a way of mercy and kindness, by fulfilling his promise, giving strength to conceive and bear a child:[119]

1 Samuel 2:21

And the LORD visited Hannah, so that she conceived, and bare three sons and two daughters. And the child Samuel grew before the LORD.

---

118 . *Thru The Bible*, volume 1, page 86.
119 . John Gill's Exposition of the Bible; http://www.ewordtoday.com/comments/genesis/gill/genesis21.htm.

The Lord did unto Sarah as he had spoken and the repetition is made to cause attention to God's fulfillment of his promise, who is always faithful to his word. Even in things very difficult and seemingly impossible, as in the present case: hence the Targums of Jonathan and Jerusalem paraphrase it, God did a wonder for Sarah in causing her to conceive when she was so old, and in such circumstances as she was.[120]

God stated in the eighteenth chapter that he would return "according to the time of life," meaning a year later when the fullness of Sarah pregnancy:

Genesis 18:14

Is any thing too hard for the LORD? At the time appointed I will return unto thee, according to the time of life, and Sarah shall have a son.

For as Paul has written:

Galatians 4:4

But when the fulness of the time was come, God sent forth his Son, made of a woman, made under the law,

Circumcision of Isaac
Verse 4

Following the command of God, Abraham circumcised his son Isaac, being eight days old, and not a day before or after.

Genesis 17:12

And he that is eight days old shall be circumcised among you, every man child in your generations, he that is born in the house, or bought with money of any stranger, which is not of thy seed.

Abraham's action shows his strict regard and ready obedience to satisfy the demands and wishes of God.

Recent studies have confirmed that the safest time to perform a circumcision is on the eighth day of life. Vitamin K, which causes blood to coagulate, is not produced in

---

120   . John Gill's Exposition of the Bible; http://www.ewordtoday.com/comments/genesis/gill/genesis21.htm.

sufficient amounts until the fifth to seventh day. On the eighth day, the body contains 10% more prothrombin than normal; prothrombin is also important in the clotting of blood.[121]

Sarah Laughed
Verses 6–7

Sarah is filled with joy in verse 6: *God hath made me to laugh*; he has given her both cause to rejoice and a heart to rejoice. Further, Sarah invites all to rejoice with her, as God has shown mercy and fulfilled her heart's desire. Others would rejoice at the witnessing of God's power and goodness, and be encouraged to trust in Him.[122] The psalmist puts it this way:

Psalm 119:74
> They that fear thee will be glad when they see me; because I have hoped in thy word.

In verse 7, Sarah is filed with awl and wonder; at age ninety, she has given birth to a son and is all the more able to breastfeed her son. Who would have thought she would ever have a child, much less say to Abraham what a son Sarah has given you. The wonder of her being pregnant, which is improbable, if not impossible, but for the omnipotent God Yahweh, nothing is impossible.

Note:
> The birth of Isaac is God preparing man for the supernatural workings of his hand that will lead to the miraculous birth of Chris Jesus. Thus, God started from the beginning with two people long past the stage of life for child rearing let alone propagating one. The birth of Isaac really had nothing to do with Sarah and Abraham; they are merely the vessels God had chosen some twenty-five years earlier.[123]

---

121 . *Illustrated Manners and Customs of the Bible*, 1980, page 448.
122 . Matthew Henry's Commentary, volume 1, page.
123 . *Thru The Bible*, volume 1, page 86.

Isaac Is Weaned
Verse 8

Isaac was two to three years old when he was weaned. In ancient Jewish and even today in some Mideastern culture, mothers will continue to nurse the child until they are two or three years old. At that time, they are weaned and would cross the line separating infancy from childhood.[124] The neighbors where invited; there is the likelihood Abimelech also.

The weaning occasioned a feast (party) to celebrate the crossing from infant to child. Training of Isaac would now commence, and the teacher is his father, Abraham. As Isaac is the child of promise, Abraham is ecstatic and the feast was something. We can only imagine the food:

Luke 15:23
> And bring hither the fatted calf, and kill it; and let us eat, and be merry.

After all Isaac was the child God promised Sarah and Abraham, and out of his lineage, the entire world shall be blessed. From this lineage came the savior of the world Christ Jesus, and a celebration is required.

EXPULSION OF HAGAR AND ISHMAEL
Genesis 21:9–21

9. *And Sarah saw the son of Hagar the Egyptian, which she had born unto Abraham, mocking.*
10. *Wherefore she said unto Abraham, Cast out this bondwoman and her son: for the son of this bondwoman shall not be heir with my son, even with Isaac.*
11. *And the thing was very grievous in Abraham's sight because of his son.*
12. *And God said unto Abraham, Let it not be grievous in thy sight because of the lad, and because of thy bondwoman; in all that Sarah hath said unto thee, hearken unto her voice; for in Isaac shall thy seed be called.*
13. *And also of the son of the bondwoman will I make a nation, because he is thy seed.*

---

124   *. Illustrated Manners and Customs of the Bible*, 1980, page 449.

14. *And Abraham rose up early in the morning, and took bread, and a bottle of water, and gave it unto Hagar, putting it on her shoulder, and the child, and sent her away: and she departed, and wandered in the wilderness of Beersheba.*

15. *And the water was spent in the bottle, and she cast the child under one of the shrubs.*

16. *And she went, and sat her down over against him a good way off, as it were a bow shot: for she said, Let me not see the death of the child. And she sat over against him, and lift up her voice, and wept.*

17. *And God heard the voice of the lad; and the angel of God called to Hagar out of heaven, and said unto her, What aileth thee, Hagar? fear not; for God hath heard the voice of the lad where he is.*

18. *Arise, lift up the lad, and hold him in thine hand; for I will make him a great nation.*

19. *And God opened her eyes, and she saw a well of water; and she went, and filled the bottle with water, and gave the lad drink.*

20. *And God was with the lad; and he grew, and dwelt in the wilderness, and became an archer.*

21. *And he dwelt in the wilderness of Paran: and his mother took him a wife out of the land of Egypt.*

Ishmael Mocks Isaac
Verses 9–13

Ishmael is about seventeen years of age and is mocking Isaac, age 2 or 3. Witnessed by Sarah and was provoked to anger, because she did not want Ishmael to share as heir with her son Isaac.

The word *mocking*, the Greek verb *diōkō* or Hebrew verb *sāhaq* has several meanings, for example: When Joseph rejected her, Potiphar's wife complains that her husband brought the Hebrew slave into their house "to insult us" (NRSV), "to mock us" (KJV), "to make sport of us" (NIV).[125] This verb can refer to the following:

children playing

---

125   . Isaac Born, Ishmael Banished by Dr. Ralph F. Wilson, http://www.jesuswalk.com/abraham/9_birth.htm.

Zechariah 8:5,

> And the streets of the city shall be full of boys and girls *playing* in the streets thereof.

tambourines and dancing

1 Samuel 18:6–7

6. And it came to pass as they came, when David was returned from the slaughter of the Philistine, that the women came out of all cities of Israel, singing and dancing, to meet king Saul, with tabrets, with joy, and with instruments of musick.

7. And the women answered one another as they played, and said, Saul hath slain his thousands, and David his ten thousands.

or to celebrate

1 Samuel 6:5, 21

5. And David and all the house of Israel played before the LORD on all manner of instruments made of fir wood, even on harps, and on psalteries, and on timbrels, and on cornets, and on cymbals.

21. And David said unto Michal, It was before the LORD, which chose me before thy father, and before all his house, to appoint me ruler over the people of the LORD, over Israel: therefore will I play before the LORD.

In our passage, there seems to be two possibilities:[126]

1. Sarah sees Ishmael **playing** with her son, as if he's one of the family, and becomes enraged that he *is* a member of the family. The NRSV's translation "playing with her son Isaac" draws on the Septuagint and Vulgate translations that include the words "with her son Isaac," which are missing in the Hebrew Masoretic text.

2. Sarah sees Ishmael **mocking** or making fun of Isaac—or maybe even hurting Isaac—and becomes enraged that this son of a servant girl is bothering her son, Abraham's heir. Paul says that Ishmael "persecuted" Isaac, perhaps referring to this incident—whether by verbal or physical abuse, we don't know.

---

126   . Isaac Born, Ishmael Banished by Dr. Ralph F. Wilson, http://www.jesuswalk.com/abraham/9_birth.htm,

Galatians 4:29

> But as then he that was born after the flesh persecuted him that was born after the Spirit, even so it is now.

The Hammurabi Code states that the son of a slave woman could claim a share of the father's property:

> If his wife bear sons to a man, or his maid-servant have borne sons, and the father while still living says to the children whom his maid servant has borne: "My sons," and he count them with the sons of his wife; if then the father die, then the sons of the wife and of the maid servant shall divide the paternal property in common. The son of the wife is to partition and choose.[127]

The Code of Hammurabi is a well-preserved Babylonian law code, dating to ca. 1780 BC. It is one of the oldest deciphered writings of significant length in the world. The sixth Babylonian king, Hammurabi, enacted the code, and partial copies exist on a human-sized stone *stele* and various clay tablets. The Code consists of 282 laws, with scaled punishments, adjusting "an eye for an eye, a tooth for a tooth" (*lex talionis*) as graded depending on social status, of slave versus free man.

Nearly one-half of the Code deals with matters of contract, establishing for example the wages to be paid to an ox driver or a surgeon. Other provisions set the terms of a transaction, establishing the Code on diorite stele[128] liability of a builder for a house that collapses, for example, or property that is damaged while left in the care of another.

A third of the code addresses issues concerning household and family relationships such as inheritance, divorce, paternity, and sexual behavior. Only one provision appears to impose obligations on an official; this provision establishes that a judge who reaches an incorrect decision is to be fined and removed from the bench permanently. A handful of provisions address issues related to military service.

---

127   http://www.takdangaralin.com/history/code-of-hammurabi/the-code-of-hammurabi-121-to-170/,

128   Code of Hammurabi , Palais Royal, Musée du Louvre, 75001 Paris, France; http://en.wikipedia.org/wiki/File:Code_of_Hammurabi.jpg.

KEN FOOKES

Based on the provision of the Hammurabi Code, Sarah was anxious for her son Isaac's inheritance, and if Ishmael would have been allowed to remain within the family as firstborn may have inherited all. Placing this demand on Abraham by Sarah means there is only one son, Isaac.

Cast out this bondwoman and her son: Sarah saw plainly that there would be neither peace nor comfort for her and her son, unless Hagar and her son are turned out.[129] This is true to this very day, the conflict between the Arabs and Israel by the Arabs' surrogate the Palestinian is a continuation of this family feud. Therefore, she demands that Abraham put them out of their home.

Very grievous in Abraham's sight: Abraham is devastated, his heart is breaking. Sarah has caused to experience emotional pain at the loss of his seventeen-year-old son. He has watched Ishmael develop into a young man and has seen him as his heir, but Sarah is determined to have Abraham submit to her desire and put out Hagar the Egyptian bondwoman and her son Ishmael.[130] They are separated from the Abrahamic family, and go their own way. It is the sentence passed on all sinners; they may be members of the visible church, but are born of the flesh and not born again, those that rest in the law and reject the message of grace through Christ Jesus, shall most certainly be case out.[131]

Galatians 4:22–23, 30
22. For it is written, that Abraham had two sons, the one by a bondmaid, the other by a freewoman.
23. But he who was of the bondwoman was born after the flesh; but he of the freewoman was by promise.
30. Nevertheless what saith the scripture? Cast out the bondwoman and her son: for the son of the bondwoman shall not be heir with the son of the freewoman.

The demand that Sarah made is not a result of her desire for her son to be sole heir, but is divinely directed by God, as is evident from God's approbation of it in verse 12. For God spoke to Abraham, saying, "Let it not be grievous in thy sight because

129   . John Gill's Exposition of the Bible; http://www.ewordtoday.com/comments/genesis/gill/genesis21.htm.
130   . Isaac Born, Ishmael Banished by Dr. Ralph F. Wilson; http://www.jesuswalk.com/abraham/9_birth.htm.
131   . Matthew Henry's Commentary, volume 1, page 107.

of the lad, and because of the bondwoman." That is, do not let Sarah demand upset you, to turn out the bondwoman and her son, and do not let your love for them hinder compliance of her desire. What Sarah has said is not evil, but the correct and proper thing to do, and leave the bondwoman and her son to me; I will take care of them, be under no concern for them and their welfare.[132]

In verse 13, God tells Abraham that out of Ishmael will come a nation, because he is the son of Abraham. In chapter 20, this promise was made to Hagar and on page 146 the son are listed. We know this to be true today for the Ishmaelites or Arabs are the King and potentates of that region of the world.

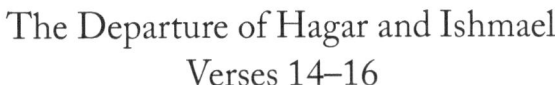

The Departure of Hagar and Ishmael
Verses 14–16

Abraham Case out Hagar and Ishmael[133]

Upon arising early in the morning, Abraham, in obedience to the word of God, prepared the meagerness of provision, a skin of water and bread. As Abraham loved his son, he could have provided so much more: animals to carry the supplies, but he

---

132 . John Gill's Exposition of the Bible; http://www.cwordtoday.com/comments/genesis/gill/genesis21.htm.
133 . http://www.preaching.com/sermons/11563848/.

only provided bread and water, the very minimum to sustain life. Why would he be so sparing in providing the supplies they would require: there was no tent for shelter, no beast of burden, no servants, and insufficient food. What follows are a few possible answers as to why.

Matthew Henry suggests, "If Hagar and Ishmael had conducted themselves well in Abraham's family, they might have continued there; but they threw themselves out by their own pride and insolence, which were thus justly chastised."[134]

John Gill put fore the following: "He was to hearken in this affair to whatsoever Sarah said, and act accordingly, perhaps this was all she would grant; or it might be so ordered by the providence of God, as a chastisement for their ill behavior, and that they might know the difference between being in Abraham's house and out of it."[135]

Here is one last possibility: Abraham being a man of faith knows that God had stated He would make a nation out of Ishmael; therefore, God shall be their provider—El Shaddai (see pages 63 and 64 for an explanation of El Shaddai).

Now Abraham put the provisions on her shoulders, delivered Ishmael into her hand, to be cared for by her; and very probably she led him in her hand. She departed and wandered in the wilderness of Beersheba. This is the place Abraham had left, following the conflagration of the cities of the plain, and this might be the birthplace of Isaac.

Apparently, she had no concept of survival on her own for she and Ishmael have consumed their skimpy provisions and cannot live off the land. As a slave, she was accustomed to being cared for, told what and what not to do, and having her needs provided by the master.

With the meager resources spent, Ishmael exhausted and parched, his mother laid him under, in the words of rabbis, juniper trees to shade him from the scorching sun and she leaves him there to die. Hagar not wanting to witness the death of her child, when *as it were a bow shot* distant; about as far off from him as an arrow can be shot, or is usually shot out of a bow; according to the Jews this was about half a mile, for they say two bowshots make a mile. Here she sat waiting what would be the issue, whether life

---

134   . Matthew Henry's Commentary, volume 1, page 108.
135   . John Gill's Exposition of the Bible; http://www.ewordtoday.com/comments/genesis/gill/genesis21.htm.

or death, which last she expected. She lifted up her voice and wept, on account of her desolate and forlorn condition. She could get no water, and her child, as she thought, dying with thirst.[136]

Angel Assists Hagar and Ishmael
Verses17–21

This is the second time that an angel of the Lord speaks to Hagar to protect her and Ishmael (see 16:7–12). This time the angel tells her not to be afraid, that God has heard the boy's voice. That she is not to quit, but to pick up her son and take him by the hand. Then her eyes are opened to see a well in the middle of the desert. Where death and desolation was all she could see a minute before, now she sees hope. God promises a future for Ishmael, and God provides the sustenance they need to survive.

Growing up in the desert or wilderness may seem like a bleak prospect to you, but as part of Abraham's household, Hagar and Ishmael have been encamped at the edge of the desert for years. If they have water, they will learn how to survive. Mother and nearly grown son now begin a life in the wilderness of Paran. This location seems to be in the northeast section of the Sinai Peninsula, southwest of Edom and south of the wilderness of Zin near the Judean mountains, but as far north as Kadesh or even Beer-sheba (see pages 25-26).

136   . John Gill's Exposition of the Bible; http://www.ewordtoday.com/comments/genesis/gill/genesis21.htm.

Hagar in the Wilderness[137]

Ishmael grows to manhood in the desert and becomes a skilled archer, no doubt killing small animals that provide clothing and food for them. When he is older, Hagar returns to her native Egypt and finds a wife for her son.[138]

ABRAHAM AND ABIMELECH MAKE A TREATY
Genesis 21:22–32

22. *And it came to pass at that time, that Abimelech and Phichol the chief captain of his host spake unto Abraham, saying, God is with thee in all that thou doest:*
23. *Now therefore swear unto me here by God that thou wilt not deal falsely with me, nor with my son, nor with my son's son: but according to the kindness that I have done unto thee, thou shalt do unto me, and to the land wherein thou hast sojourned.*
24. *And Abraham said, I will swear.*
25. *And Abraham reproved Abimelech because of a well of water, which Abimelech's servants had violently taken away.*

---

137   . Jean Baptiste Camille Corot 1835; http://freechristimages.org/biblestories/hagar_and_the_angel.htm.
138   . Isaac Born, Ishmael Banished by Dr. Ralph F. Wilson; http://www.jesuswalk.com/abraham/9_birth.htm.

26. *And Abimelech said, I wot not who hath done this thing; neither didst thou tell me, neither yet heard I of it, but to day.*

27. *And Abraham took sheep and oxen, and gave them unto Abimelech; and both of them made a covenant.*

28. *And Abraham set seven ewe lambs of the flock by themselves.*

29. *And Abimelech said unto Abraham, What mean these seven ewe lambs which thou hast set by themselves?*

30. *And he said, For these seven ewe lambs shalt thou take of my hand, that they may be a witness unto me, that I have digged this well.*

31. *Wherefore he called that place Beersheba; because there they sware both of them.*

32. *Thus they made a covenant at Beersheba: then Abimelech rose up, and Phichol the chief captain of his host, and they returned into the land of the Philistines.*

Treaty Between Abimelech and Abraham
Verses 22–24

We have here an account of the treaty between Abimelech and Abraham, in which appears the accomplishment of that promise (chapter 12:2) that God would *make his name great.* His friendship is valued, is courted, though a stranger, though a tenant at will to the Canaanites and Perizzites.[139]

Abimelech was king of Gerar, and Phichol was the general of his army; these two great personages came together and paid Abraham a visit. The conversation was brought about due to their observations of *"God is with thee in all that thou doest."* They saw that he increased in worldly substance, and that his family was increased, and that he succeeded in everything in which he engaged, and being jealous of his growing greatness and power, were desirous of securing an interest in him and in his favor.[140] God in his providence sometimes shows his people such tokens for good that their neighbors cannot but take notice of it:[141]

Psalm 86:17

Shew me a token for good; that they which hate me may see it, and be ashamed: because thou, LORD, hast helped me, and comforted me.

---

139 . Matthew Henry's Commentary, volume 1, page 109.
140 . John Gill's Exposition of the Bible; http://www.ewordtoday.com/comments/genesis/gill/genesis21.htm.
141 . Matthew Henry's Commentary, volume 1, page 109; from this point to the end of this section.

It is good being in favor with those that are in favour with God, and having an interest in those that have an interest in heaven:

Zechariah 8:23

> Thus saith the LORD of hosts; In those days it shall come to pass, that ten men shall take hold out of all languages of the nations, even shall take hold of the skirt of him that is a Jew, saying, We will go with you: for we have heard that God is with you.

We do well for ourselves if we have fellowship with those that have fellowship with God:

1 John 1:3
> That which we have seen and heard declare we unto you, that ye also may have fellowship with us: and truly our fellowship is with the Father, and with his Son Jesus Christ.

.

The tenor of it was that there should be a firm and constant friendship between the two families, which should not upon any account be violated. This bond of friendship must be strengthened by the bond of an oath, in which the true God was appealed to, both as a witness of their sincerity and an avenger in case either side were treacherous. Abimelech's desires are that this treaty extend to his posterity and the extension of it to his people. He would have his son, and his son's son, and his land likewise, to have the benefit of it. Good men should secure an alliance and communion with the favorites of heaven, not for themselves only, but for theirs also. To further convince Abraham that he should, Abimelech reminds Abraham of his kindness he has shown him. Therefore, they enter into this covenant, and they swear an oath of confirmation.

Question of Well Ownership
Verses 25–32

Abraham brings up a sore subject for him, the well he has dug, and Abimelech states this the first he has heard of this. In the Septuagint version, well is in the plural form "the wells":

Genesis 26:15

> For all the wells which his father's servants had digged in the days of Abraham his father, the Philistines had stopped them, and filled them with earth.

Abraham is a very honorable man, for he take sheep and oxen giving them to Abimelech in gratitude for past favors and as a token of friendship. His action proved to Abimelech that his answer was fully satisfying. Further, the animals present Abraham willingness to enter into covenant by sacrifice, or cut or struck a covenant. The creatures were divided, and the covenanters passed between the pieces, and both of them made a covenant; or "cut or struck a covenant"; cut the sacrifice in pieces and passed between them, in token of the compact and agreement they entered into with each other, signifying that whoever broke it deserved to be cut in pieces as those creatures were.

Abimelech acknowledged by his acceptance of these seven lambs that well is Abraham. It is very probably Abraham received a note from the hand of Abimelech, owning his reception of the seven lambs, and his title to the well, which these were a witness of.

The place being named Beersheba, "Beer" signifying a well, and "sheba" seven, thus the name means the well of seven lambs. Once the agreement and the ceremony completed, Abimelech and Phichol returned to the capital city of Gerar in the land of the Philistines. Beersheba is a large village, twenty miles from Hebron to the south.[142]

ABRAHAM WORSHIPED GOD
Genesis 21:33–34

> *33. And Abraham planted a grove in Beersheba, and called there on the name of the LORD, the everlasting God.*
> *34. And Abraham sojourned in the Philistin*

Abraham, having got into a good neighborhood, knew when he was well off and continued a great while there. There he planted a grove for a shade to his tent, or perhaps an orchard of fruit trees; and there, though we cannot say he settled, for God would have him, while he lived, to be a stranger and a pilgrim, yet he sojourned many days, as many as would consist with his character, as Abraham the *Hebrew*, or *passenger*. There

---

142 . John Gill's Exposition of the Bible; http://www.ewordtoday.com/comments/genesis/gill/genesis21.htm.

he made, not only a constant practice, but an open profession, of his religion: *There he called on the name of the Lord, the everlasting God,* probably in the grove he planted, which was his oratory or house of prayer. Christ prayed in a garden, on a mountain. (1) Abraham kept up public worship, to which, probably, his neighbors resorted, that they might join with him. Note, Good men should not only retain their goodness wherever they go, but do all they can to propagate it, and make others good. (2) In calling on the Lord, we must eye him as *the everlasting God, the God of the world,* so some. Though God had made himself known to Abraham as his God in particular, and in covenant with him, yet he forgets not to give glory to him as the Lord of all: *The everlasting God,* who was, before all worlds, and will be, when time and days shall be no more.[143]

Isaiah 40:28

> Hast thou not known? hast thou not heard, that the everlasting God, the LORD, the Creator of the ends of the earth, fainteth not, neither is weary? there is no searching of his understanding.

The rabbis say that Abraham remained in the area of Beersheba about twenty-six years.

---

143 . Matthew Henry's Commentary, volume 1, page 109.

SACRIFICE OF ISAAC
Genesis 22

Abraham and Isaac[144]

CHAPTER OVERVIEW

This chapter Moses tells of the most memorable narrative of the Old Testament, the testing of Abraham by the Almighty. This is a trial that most if not all believers would fail, for whom among us would sacrifice one's child? Matthew Henry says, "Every trial is indeed a temptation, and tends to show the dispositions of the heart, whether holy or unholy. But God proved Abraham, not to draw him to sin, as Satan tempts. Strong faith is often exercised with strong trials, and put upon hard services."[145]

---

144   . http://www.oneil.com.au/lds/pictures/abraham.jpg.
145   . Matthew Henry's Commentary, volume 1, page 109.

CHAPTER STRUCTURE

- God commands Abraham to sacrifice Isaac. (1–2)
- Abraham obeys the Divine command. (3–10)
- The Almighty provides the sacrifice (11–14)
- The covenant with Abraham renewed. (15–19)
- The sons of Nahor the brother of Abraham. (20–24)

GOD COMMANDS ABRAHAM TO SACRIFICE ISAAC
Genesis 22:1–2

1. *And it came to pass after these things, that God did tempt Abraham, and said unto him, Abraham: and he said, Behold, here I am.*
2. *And he said, Take now thy son, thine only son Isaac, whom thou lovest, and get thee into the land of Moriah; and offer him there for a burnt offering upon one of the mountains which I will tell thee of.*

And it came to pass after these things, this phraseology calls to mind all that Abraham and Sarah have gone through. From being called by God to leave Ur and then his departure from Haran, then the sojourn across Canaan into Egypt and the denial of Sarah as his wife; the return to Canaan, the rescue of Lot, the blood covenant God made with Abraham, and the birth of Ishmael. There is the promise of Isaac born of Sarah followed by the destruction of the cities of the plain; the birth of Isaac, then the weaning of Isaac celebration, and the putting out of Hagar and her teenage son Ishmael, and finally the treaty between Abimelech and Abraham.

In verse 1, Moses uses the phrase *that God did tempt Abraham*, however in the book of James chapter 1 and verse 13, we read:

Let no man say when he is tempted, I am tempted of God: for God cannot be tempted with evil, neither tempteth he any man:

However, our Lord God does provide opportunities for our faith to grown and to witness His awesome power, honor, and glory as depicted in the scriptures:

1 Corinthians 10:13

> There hath no temptation taken you but such as is common to man: but God is faithful, who will not suffer you to be tempted above that ye are able; but will with the temptation also make a way to escape, that ye may be able to bear it.

1 Peter 1:7

> That the trial of your faith, being much more precious than of gold that perisheth, though it be tried with fire, might be found unto praise and honour and glory at the appearing of Jesus Christ:

God calls out to Abraham and he responds, "*Behold, here I am*" or look at me I'm standing here! Another though, I'm here at your command, or as you will I shall do. This is the attitude we should all have, for we are but the creature not on the same plane as the creator.

Notice in verse 2 how God causes Abraham to recall not only who Isaac is, but the depth of emotional ties between Abraham and Isaac. For Isaac is the son of promise whom Abraham waited some twenty-five years; from the time God first promise till fulfillment. Why would God do so? In this way God has intensified the testing of Abraham. This test of faith is answered by Abraham in verse 8.

God tells him to take his son to *the land of Moriah*, which literally means "chosen by Jehovah."[146] The mount on the eastern edge of Jerusalem on which Solomon built the temple, or today known as the temple mount. Thus the reader is to understand that God chose the city of Jerusalem. As spoken of in scripture:

2 Chronicles 3:1

> Then Solomon began to build the house of the LORD at Jerusalem in mount Moriah, where the Lord appeared unto David his father, in the place that David had prepared in the threshingfloor of Ornan the Jebusite.

And offer him there for a burnt offering: Can you imagine what must have been going on in the mind of Abraham? Because of his faith, was he thinking God will resurrect Isaac, or as he stated in verse 8, God *will provide himself a lamb for a burnt offering*?

---

146   . http://www.biblestudytools.com/search/?q=Moriah&s=References&rc=LEX&rc2=LEX+HEB.

ABRAHAM OBEYS THE DIVINE COMMAND
Genesis 22:3–10

3. *And Abraham rose up early in the morning, and saddled his ass, and took two of his young men with him, and Isaac his son, and clave the wood for the burnt offering, and rose up, and went unto the place of which God had told him.*

4. *Then on the third day Abraham lifted up his eyes, and saw the place afar off.*

5. *And Abraham said unto his young men, Abide ye here with the ass; and I and the lad will go yonder and worship, and come again to you.*

6. *And Abraham took the wood of the burnt offering, and laid it upon Isaac his son; and he took the fire in his hand, and a knife; and they went both of them together.*

7. *And Isaac spake unto Abraham his father, and said, My father: and he said, Here am I, my son. And he said, Behold the fire and the wood: but where is the lamb for a burnt offering?*

8. *And Abraham said, My son, God will provide himself a lamb for a burnt offering: so they went both of them together.*

9. *And they came to the place which God had told him of; and Abraham built an altar there, and laid the wood in order, and bound Isaac his son, and laid him on the altar upon the wood.*

10. *And Abraham stretched forth his hand, and took the knife to slay his son.*

Verse 3 tells us that Abraham was a man of absolute obedience to God's instruction. Upon receiving God's command to offer up Isaac as a sacrifice, he *rose up early in the morning* and got on with the task at hand. He did not procrastinate, debate, or ask for an explanation, just one of complete submission.

From verse 4, the reader will note that it was a three-day trek from Beersheba to Moriah, for on the third day Abraham *saw the place afar off.* It is hard to imagine the anguish Abraham must have been going through knowing what was coming. There is a parallel with the three days that Christ Jesus was in the grave. The similarities will become clearer as we proceed through these verses.

Abraham now tells the young men that accompany them to wait for them, placing the wood on Isaac's back to carry. This again is very similar to Christ Jesus carrying the cross to Calvary, and in fact biblical scholars have often identified Calvary and mount Moriah as one and the same; however, this interpretation is in dispute.

John 19:17

>And he bearing his cross went forth into a place called the place of a skull, which is called in the Hebrew Golgotha:

In verse 8 Abraham shows himself to be a man of true faith, when asked by Isaac where is the lamb, Abraham states that God would provide the lamb.

Abraham and Isaac[147]

Hebrews 11:17–18
17. By faith Abraham, when he was tried, offered up Isaac: and he that had received the promises offered up his only begotten son,
18. Of whom it was said, That in Isaac shall thy seed be called

Revelation 5:6
And I beheld, and, lo, in the midst of the throne and of the four beasts, and in the midst of the elders, stood a **Lamb** as it had **been slain**, having seven horns and seven eyes, which are the seven Spirits of God sent forth into all the earth.

His response points to Christ Jesus and the cross, although unbeknownst to Abraham. We on the other hand have the advantage of hindsight and can see this clearly as we read this chapter.

Abraham in verse 9 builds the altar and then arranges the wood, and then the most interesting part of the narrative. Isaac at this point is not a child, but a young man of

---

147   . http://derekspain.files.wordpress.com/2011/07/abraham-and-isaac.jpg.

somewhere between 18 and 30[148] years of age. Just as Christ Jesus willingly went to the cross, Isaac likewise willingly was bound and laid upon the altar.

Luke 22:42

> Saying, Father, if thou be willing, remove this cup from me: nevertheless not my will, but thine, be done.

Verse 10 we read that Abraham is preparing to sacrifice Isaac.

THE ALMIGHTY PROVIDES THE SACRIFICE
Genesis 22:11–14

The *Sacrifice of Isaac*[149]

> *11. And the angel of the LORD called unto him out of heaven, and said, Abraham, Abraham: and he said, Here am I.*

---

148   . Sarah dies at the age of 127 (genesis 23:1), Isaac is age 37, and this narrative between chapters 21 and 23 is period of approximately 37 years. Basing this assertion on the intervals that God appears to Abraham of 13 to 25 years, and Isaac weaning celebration of age 5 that provides a range of 18 to 30 years for Isaac's age.

149   . http://1.bp.blogspot.com/-nBNF8KhI4ds/TVMnCAiXjMI/AAAAAAAACYQ/x_reeDs5Kfo/s1600/028%2B-%2BAbraham%2BSacrifices%2BIsaac.gif.

12. *And he said, Lay not thine hand upon the lad, neither do thou any thing unto him: for now I know that thou fearest God, seeing thou hast not withheld thy son, thine only son from me.*

13. *And Abraham lifted up his eyes, and looked, and behold behind him a ram caught in a thicket by his horns: and Abraham went and took the ram, and offered him up for a burnt offering in the stead of his son.*

14. *And Abraham called the name of that place Jehovahjireh: as it is said to this day, In the mount of the LORD it shall be seen.*

In this section of the narrative, Abraham is prevented by the *angel of the LORD* (a Christophany) from sacrificing his son Isaac. Abraham's willingness to sacrifice his son Isaac is proof of his love and trust in God. God indeed provides a ram for the burnt offering; therefore, Abraham calls the place Jehovahjireh, meaning God will provide.[150]

THE COVENANT WITH ABRAHAM RENEWED
Genesis 22:15–19

15. *And the angel of the LORD called unto Abraham out of heaven the second time,*

16. *And said, By myself have I sworn, saith the LORD, for because thou hast done this thing, and hast not withheld thy son, thine only son:*

17. *That in blessing I will bless thee, and in multiplying I will multiply thy seed as the stars of the heaven, and as the sand which is upon the sea shore; and thy seed shall possess the gate of his enemies;*

18. *And in thy seed shall all the nations of the earth be blessed; because thou hast obeyed my voice.*

19. *So Abraham returned unto his young men, and they rose up and went together to Beersheba; and Abraham dwelt at Beersheba.*

God is so pleased with Abraham that He not only renews his covenant, but delineates the details of the blessing:

- *in blessing I will bless thee*
  Abraham was blessed with peaceful long healthy life and wealth,
- *in multiplying I will multiply thy seed as the stars of the heaven, and as the sand which is upon the seashore*

---

150   . http://www.biblestudytools.com/search/?q=Jehovahjireh&s=References.

This blessing has been fulfilled for there are Hebrews in every corner of the world, being more numerous than one can count.

- *and thy seed shall possess the gate of his enemies*
  History will attest to this blessing, and in modern times the world has watched as the small nation of Israel has defeated those aggressor nations surrounding Israel.

- *in thy seed shall all the nations of the earth be blessed*
  It is through the Hebrews of the tribe Judea and lineage of King David that the redeemer of the world Christ Jesus descent.
  The majority of the Nobel laureates are Hebrew/Jewish heritage in a variety of disciplines: medicine, mathematics, physics, chemistry, etc.

THE SONS OF NAHOR, THE BROTHER OF ABRAHAM
Genesis 22:20–24

20. *And it came to pass after these things, that it was told Abraham, saying, Behold, Milcah, she hath also born children unto thy brother Nahor;*
21. *Huz his firstborn, and Buz his brother, and Kemuel the father of Aram,*
22. *And Chesed, and Hazo, and Pildash, and Jidlaph, and Bethuel.*
23. *And Bethuel begat Rebekah: these eight Milcah did bear to Nahor, Abraham's brother.*
24. *And his concubine, whose name was Reumah, she bare also Tebah, and Gaham, and Thahash, and Maachah.*

This chapter ends with some account of Nahor's family, who had settled at Haran. This seems to be given for the connection which it had with the God's chosen. From thence Isaac and Jacob took wives; and before the account of those events, this list is recorded. It shows that though Abraham saw his own family highly honored with privileges, admitted into covenant, and blessed with the assurance of the promise, yet he did not look with disdain upon his relations, but was glad to hear of the increase and welfare of their families.[151]

---

151 . Matthew Henry Commentary, volume 1, page 111.

Nahor's Descendants				
Wife	Children	Grandchildren	Concubine	Children
Milcah			Reumah	
	Huz			Tebah
	Buz			Gaham
	Kemuel	Aram		Thahash
	Chesed			Maachah
	Hazo			
	Pildash			
	Jidlaph			
	Bethuel	Rebekah*		

*Rebekah is to be the wife of Isaac:

Genesis 24:4, 15, 50–51

4. But thou shalt go unto my country, and to my kindred, and take a wife unto my son Isaac.

15. And it came to pass, before he had done speaking, that, behold, Rebekah came out, who was born to Bethuel, son of Milcah, the wife of Nahor, Abraham's brother, with her pitcher upon her shoulder.

50. Then Laban and Bethuel answered and said, The thing proceedeth from the LORD: we cannot speak unto thee bad or good.

51. Behold, Rebekah is before thee, take her, and go, and let her be thy master's son's wife, as the LORD hath spoken

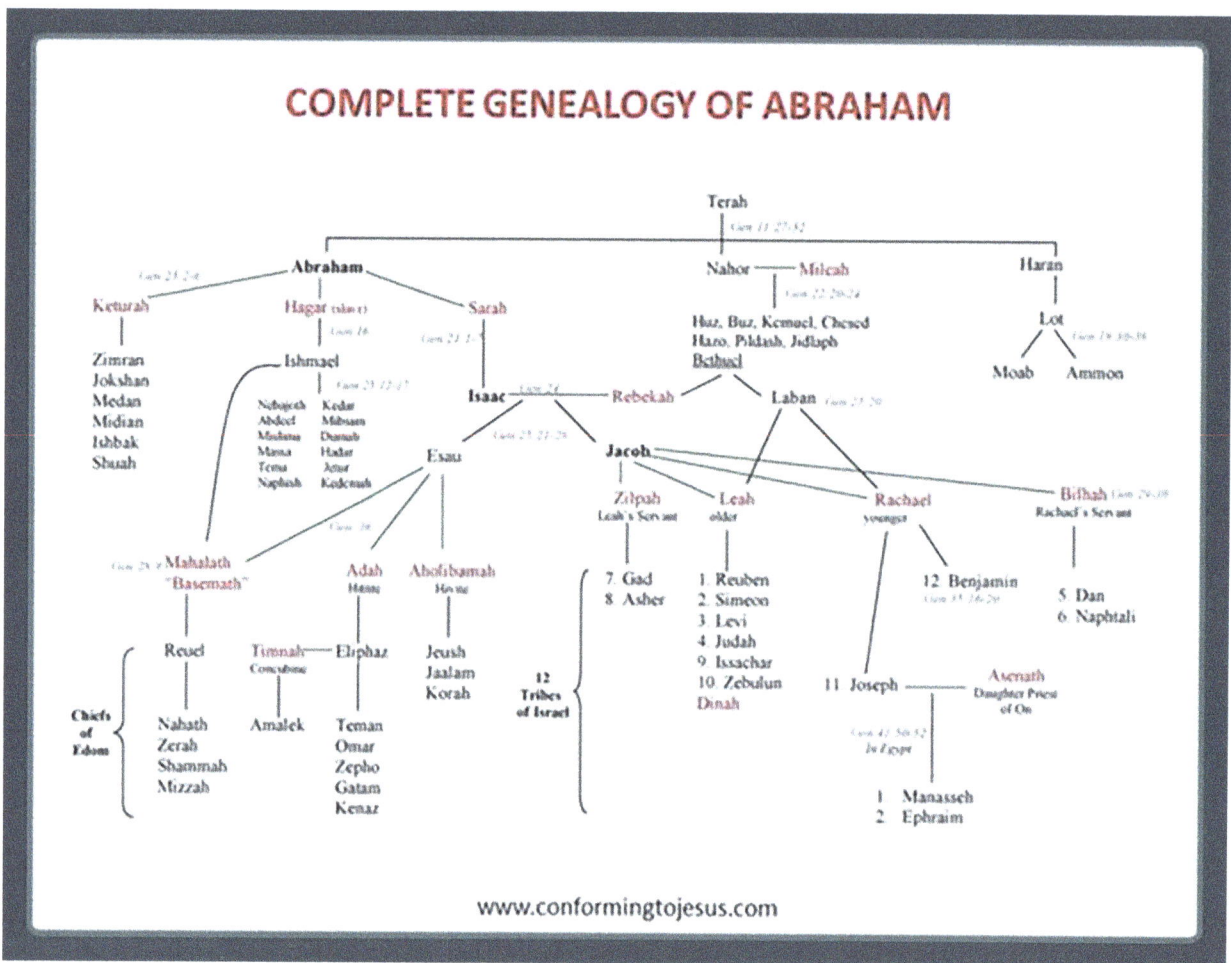

Genealogy of Abraham[153]

THE DEATH OF SARAH

Genesis 23

Burial of Sarah[152]

CHAPTER OVERVIEW

In this chapter, the death and burial of Sarah is recorded. Abraham mourns her death and negotiates with the sons of Heth for a parcel of land to bury his wife Sarah.

---

152   . *Burial of Sarah* by Tom Lovell (American illustrator (1909–1997), for *Everyday Life in Bible Times* (National Geographic Society, 1967), p. 104–105: www.jesuswalk.com/abraham/11_death.htm.

CHAPTER STRUCTURE

- Abraham mourns the death of Sarah (1–2)
- Abraham negotiates a parcel of land (3–13)
- Abraham purchases a parcel of land (14–18)
- Abraham buries Sarah (19–20)

ABRAHAM MOURNS THE DEATH OF SARAH
Genesis 23:1–2

1. *And Sarah was an hundred and seven and twenty years old: these were the years of the life of Sarah.*
2. *And Sarah died in Kirjatharba; the same is Hebron in the land of Canaan: and Abraham came to mourn for Sarah, and to weep for her.*

This is the first mention of Sarah following the weaning celebration about thirty-two years before; Isaac is now thirty-seven. Sarah is the only woman in the Bible whose age at death is recorded; further, she is an example of a Godly woman.[153]

Isaiah 51:1–2
1. Hearken to me, ye that follow after righteousness, ye that seek the LORD: look unto the rock whence ye are hewn, and to the hole of the pit whence ye are digged.
2. Look unto Abraham your father, and unto Sarah that bare you: for I called him alone, and blessed him, and increased him.

1 Peter 3:3–6
3. Whose adorning let it not be that outward adorning of plaiting the hair, and of wearing of gold, or of putting on of apparel;
4. But let it be the hidden man of the heart, in that which is not corruptible, even the ornament of a meek and quiet spirit, which is in the sight of God of great price.

---

153   . David Guzik's Commentaries on the Bible; http://www.studylight.org/com/guz/view. cgi?book=ge&chapter=023.

5. For after this manner in the old time the holy women also, who trusted in God, adorned themselves, being in subjection unto their own husbands:

6. Even as Sara obeyed Abraham, calling him lord: whose daughters ye are, as long as ye do well, and are not afraid with any amazement.

Sarah died in Kirjatharba; the same is Hebron in the land of Canaan: Hebron is a city in south in the mountain of Judah, approximately twenty miles south of Jerusalem and approximately twenty miles north of Beersheba and near where Abraham built an altar unto the LORD.[154]

Abraham came to mourn for Sarah: This phrase infers that Abraham was not with Sarah at the time of her death. It also infers that they moved from Beersheba or Abraham was with the flocks and herds grazing them.

Abraham came to mourn for Sarah, and to weep: Obviously he performed the applicatory ceremonies of mourning as was the custom of his day. However, his sorrow was genuine by the use of the words *mourn* and *weep*. Matthew Henry puts it this way: "He came to her tent, and sat down by the corpse, there to pay the tribute of his tears, that his eye might affect his heart, and that he might pay the greater respect to the memory of her that was gone."[155] The loss of loved ones is always intensely felt, but this is the payment for the sin of Adam and Eve—death—but by God's grace, we do have hope and as scripture affirms if you are a born again believer of Christ Jesus:

1 Thessalonians 4:13

But I would not have you to be ignorant, brethren, concerning them which are asleep, that ye sorrow not, even as others which have no hope.

ABRAHAM NEGOTIATES A PARCEL OF LAND
Genesis 23:3–13

3. *And Abraham stood up from before his dead, and spake unto the sons of Heth, saying,*

---

154   . http://www.guidedbiblestudies.com/topics/kirjatharba.htm.
155   . Matthew Henry Commentary, volume 1, page 114.

4. *I am a stranger and a sojourner with you: give me a possession of a buryingplace with you, that I may bury my dead out of my sight.*

5. *And the children of Heth answered Abraham, saying unto him,*

6. *Hear us, my lord: thou art a mighty prince among us: in the choice of our sepulchres bury thy dead; none of us shall withhold from thee his sepulchre, but that thou mayest bury thy dead.*

7. *And Abraham stood up, and bowed himself to the people of the land, even to the children of Heth.*

8. *And he communed with them, saying, If it be your mind that I should bury my dead out of my sight; hear me, and intreat for me to Ephron the son of Zohar,*

9. *That he may give me the cave of Machpelah, which he hath, which is in the end of his field; for as much money as it is worth he shall give it me for a possession of a burying place amongst you.*

10. *And Ephron dwelt among the children of Heth: and Ephron the Hittite answered Abraham in the audience of the children of Heth, even of all that went in at the gate of his city, saying,*

11. *Nay, my lord, hear me: the field give I thee, and the cave that is therein, I give it thee; in the presence of the sons of my people give I it thee: bury thy dead.*

12. *And Abraham bowed down himself before the people of the land.*

13. *And he spake unto Ephron in the audience of the people of the land, saying, But if thou wilt give it, I pray thee, hear me: I will give thee money for the field; take it of me, and I will bury my dead there.*

Spake unto the sons of Heth: Who are these people the sons of Heth? Noah's great-grandson Heth, through Ham and Canaan is the origin of the Hittites. The Hittites were an ancient nation that occupied the general area of Asia Minor and Syria. Although not as popularly well-known as other ancient empires (e.g. Egypt, Assyria, Babylon, Greece, Persia, Rome), at the peak of their power the Hittites challenged the Egyptians and Assyrians for control of what is now the land of Israel.[156] There is mention of the daughter of Heth in another four chapters:

Genesis 27:46

And Rebekah said to Isaac, I am weary of my life because of the daughters of Heth: if Jacob take a wife of the daughters of Heth, such as these which are of the daughters of the land, what good shall my life do me?

---

156   . Sons And Daughters Of Heth; by Wayne Blank; http://www.keyway.ca/htm2002/20020811.htm.

Although it is debated (among biblical scholars) whether this is a reference to real Hittites or to peoples that spoke their language.[157] These scholars can debate all they like, the Bible clearly states they are sons of Heth, and in verse 10. the passage ties the Hittites and sons of Heth as one in the same. However, this debate is outside the scope of this study guide.

Give: This is a poor translation[158] of the word "nathan" which in this case means to "sell." Therefore, Abraham is not asking them to give him the land, but to sell it to him, so let the negotiations begin. However, this is the prelude to the actual negotiations, it is a matter of good manners between the parties. This courtesy continues today in the Mideast.

Abraham begins the negotiations by stating he is not of this land but a *stranger and a sojourner*, in essence saying he realizes he is but a guest in their land. He is demonstrating the humility of the believer, for he is well respected of these people, as stated in chapter 14 of this study guide, and in verse 6, "*my lord: thou art a mighty prince among us,*" the reference to Abraham as lord and mighty prince indicate honorific epithet. He had lived among these people for sixty-two years and they knew him. Further the term mighty prince (nasi Elohim) is generally translated prince of God, thus the Hittites where acknowledging that God played mighty in Abrahams life, i.e., being divinely favored.[159] Therefore, Abraham was deeply respected and reverenced.

Abraham has this conversation in the gates of the city for this is where the elders sat an administer justice and witnessed agreements and transaction (such as the transfer of property) between individuals. Abraham beseeched the elders and specifically Ephron for the cave he owned at Machpelah.

The response of Ephron is that not the cave alone, but he must take the field as well. In accordance with Hittite law code, if Abraham only had possession of the cave then Ephron continues to be obligated for the taxes.[160] Therefore, he insisted Abraham should purchase both field and cave. Thus, Abraham says. "I'll take the field and cave; how much do you want for the field and cave?"

---

157 . The Parallel Bible Commentary; page 62.
158 . Hebrew Lexicon; http://www.biblestudytools.com/lexicons/hebrew/nas/nethan-aramaic.html.
159 . The Parallel Bible Commentary; page 62.
160 . Encyclopedia Britannica; volume 5; pages 368–370; also page 222 of this study guide.

Note:

The Hittite laws have been preserved on a number of Hittite cuneiform tablets. Cuneiform script is one of the earliest known forms of written expression. Emerging in Sumer around the thirtieth century BC, with predecessors reaching into the late fourth millennium (the Uruk IV period), cuneiform writing began as a system of pictographs. In the three millennia the script spanned, the pictorial representations became simplified and more abstract as the number of Cuneiform Tablet[161] characters in use also grew gradually smaller from about 1,000 unique characters in the Early Bronze Age to about 400 unique characters in Late Bronze Age (Hittite cuneiform).

ABRAHAM PURCHASES A PARCEL OF LAND
Genesis 23:14–18

14. *And Ephron answered Abraham, saying unto him,*
15. *My lord, hearken unto me: the land is worth four hundred shekels of silver; what is that betwixt me and thee? bury therefore thy dead.*
16. *And Abraham hearkened unto Ephron; and Abraham weighed to Ephron the silver, which he had named in the audience of the sons of Heth, four hundred shekels of silver, current money with the merchant.*
17. *And the field of Ephron which was in Machpelah, which was before Mamre, the field, and the cave which was therein, and all the trees that were in the field, that were in all the borders round about, were made sure*
18. *Unto Abraham for a possession in the presence of the children of Heth, before all that went in at the gate of his city.*

The way Ephron replies to Abraham is interesting; his wording is such that it eliminates all haggling over price. Ephron first say *the field give I thee, and the cave that is therein, I give it thee* (verse 11), but now he puts a dollar amount on the field and cave. So Abraham is now unable to dicker over the price, therefore he weighed out the amount

161   . http://en.wikipedia.org/wiki/File:Sumerian_26th_c_Adab.jpg.

of silver equaling four hundred shekels approximately 9.28 pounds[162] having a value in 2012 dollars of $2440.64.[163]

1 shekel = 10.52 grams or 0.371082 ounce[164]
0.371082 x 400 = 148.43 oz
148.43 ÷ 16 = 9.28 lbs

Silver value as of 2012
$0.58 / gram 1 shekel = 10.52 grams x 400 = $2440.64

Verses 17 and 18 are the legal descriptions of the property; by the standard of today, these are very simplistic. This verse basically outlines the transaction between Abraham and Ephron; the reader well note verse 17 states the *field of Ephron* describing the location of the property and what is contained within and on the property, much like mineral rights to property today. Verse 18 begins with *Unto Abraham*, thus passing ownership to him, as witness by the elders and all that was at the city gates conducting business. Interestingly the mentions of the trees, trees are valuable resources in this part of the world; therefore, they are cited.

Note:

> This is the actual beginning of the nation of Israel, for Abraham is father of the Hebrews/Jewish/Israelites peoples. Therefore, today when we hear Palestine claiming that the Israelites have no claim to the land, they are wrong. The location of this cave is in the town of Hebron.

ABRAHAM BURIES SARAH
Genesis 23:19–20

19. *And after this, Abraham buried Sarah his wife in the cave of the field of Machpelah before Mamre: the same is Hebron in the land of Canaan.*
20. *And the field, and the cave that is therein, were made sure unto Abraham for a possession of a buryingplace by the sons of Heth.*

---

162   . http://www.jewishvirtuallibrary.org/jsource/History/weightsandmeasures.html.
163   . http://answers.ask.com/Science/Chemistry/what_is_the_price_of_silver.
164   .http://www.metric-conversions.org/weight/grams-to-ounces.htm.

This cave became the mausoleum of the patriarchs, in addition to being the burial site for Sarah. Abraham, Isaac, Rebekah, Leah, and Jacob are also interred at this site.

Genesis 25:
8. Then Abraham gave up the ghost, and died in a good old age, an old man, and full of years; and was gathered to his people.
9. And his sons Isaac and Ishmael buried him in the cave of Machpelah, in the field of Ephron the son of Zohar the Hittite, which is before Mamre;

Genesis 49:31

There they buried Abraham and Sarah his wife; there they buried Isaac and Rebekah his wife; and there I buried Leah.

Genesis 50:7–11
7. And Joseph went up to bury his father: and with him went up all the servants of Pharaoh, the elders of his house, and all the elders of the land of Egypt,
8. And all the house of Joseph, and his brethren, and his father's house: only their little ones, and their flocks, and their herds, they left in the land of Goshen.
9. And there went up with him both chariots and horsemen: and it was a very great company.
10. And they came to the threshingfloor of Atad, which is beyond Jordan, and there they mourned with a great and very sore lamentation: and he made a mourning for his father seven days.
11. And when the inhabitants of the land, the Canaanites, saw the mourning in the floor of Atad, they said, This is a grievous mourning to the Egyptians: wherefore the name of it was called Abelmizraim, which is beyond Jordan.
12. And his sons did unto him according as he commanded them:
13. For his sons carried him into the land of Canaan, and buried him in the cave of the field of Machpelah, which Abraham bought with the field for a possession of a buryingplace of Ephron the Hittite, before Mamre.

The only exception is Rachel:

Genesis 35:19

And Rachel died, and was buried in the way to Ephrath, which is Bethlehem.

A PARTING THOUGHT

As God has promised the land to Abraham and his descendants, with the purchase of the field and burial cave, he has proven his faith. Abraham created the mausoleum of the patriarchs, thereby claiming the land as their own. With this purchase, Abraham clearly states his faith in God's promise and wants to rest in his land; he no longer was a sojourner as he was now obligated to the king to pay a land tax.

A WIFE FOR ISAAC

Genesis 24

Trek to Find a Wife[165]

CHAPTER OVERVIEW

Chapter 24 commences a major break in the second half of Genesis. We will begin the narrative of Abraham's beloved son, the son of promise, Isaac. Abraham does not want his son to marry a Canaanite woman, as Abraham had observed the Canaanite were not a Godly people but pantheistic. Therefore, he sends his chief steward, his most trusted servant, to his kinsmen in Haran and from among Isaac's cousins to fine him a bride. The fining of the wife is a demonstration of God's provision and guidance. This chapter is the longest of the patriarchal narratives and is the longest of all the

---

165   . http://themayers.com/camels/wp-content/uploads/2010/03/ken-sabuk-camels.jpg.

chapters of Genesis. Moses here records this event in a literary form, providing a hint of his education as a member of Pharaoh's house:

Acts 7:22

>And Moses was learned in all the wisdom of the Egyptians, and was mighty in words and in deeds.

This chronicle of the bride search gives a living form to the charge of:

Proverbs 3:6

>In all thy ways acknowledge him, and he shall direct thy paths.

CHAPTER STRUCTURE

- Abraham's chief steward takes an oath (1–9)
- Eliezer's Prayer (10–14)
- Meeting at the Well (15–28)
- Reaction of Laban (29–33)
- The Mission of Eliezer (34–49)
- Eliezer Has Obtained Consent (50–61)
- Consummation of the Marriage (62–67)

ABRAHAM'S CHIEF STEWARD TAKES AN OATH
Genesis 24:1–9

1. *And Abraham was old, and well stricken in age: and the LORD had blessed Abraham in all things.*
2. *And Abraham said unto his eldest servant of his house, that ruled over all that he had, Put, I pray thee, thy hand under my thigh:*
3. *And I will make thee swear by the LORD, the God of heaven, and the God of the earth, that thou shalt not take a wife unto my son of the daughters of the Canaanites, among whom I dwell:*
4. *But thou shalt go unto my country, and to my kindred, and take a wife unto my son Isaac.*

5. *And the servant said unto him, Peradventure the woman will not be willing to follow me unto this land: must I needs bring thy son again unto the land from whence thou camest?*

6. *And Abraham said unto him, Beware thou that thou bring not my son thither again.*

7. *The LORD God of heaven, which took me from my father's house, and from the land of my kindred, and which spake unto me, and that sware unto me, saying, Unto thy seed will I give this land; he shall send his angel before thee, and thou shalt take a wife unto my son from thence.*

8. *And if the woman will not be willing to follow thee, then thou shalt be clear from this my oath: only bring not my son thither again.*

9. *And the servant put his hand under the thigh of Abraham his master, and sware to him concerning that matter.*

Abraham was old, and well stricken in age: Abraham is approximately 140 years of age; the reader knows from the following:

Genesis 17:17

Then Abraham fell upon his face, and laughed, and said in his heart, Shall a child be born unto him that is an <u>hundred years old</u>? And shall Sarah, that is ninety years old, bear?

Genesis 25:20

And <u>Isaac was forty years old when he took Rebekah to wife</u>, the daughter of Bethuel the Syrian of Padanaram, the sister to Laban the Syrian.

Thus Abraham was approximately 140 years of age.

The LORD had blessed Abraham in all things: To put this statement into today's vernacular, Abraham is rich, as attested to by his steward statement:

Genesis 24:35

And the LORD hath blessed my master greatly; and he is become great: and he hath given him flocks, and herds, and silver, and gold, and menservants, and maidservants, and camels, and asses.

In verse 2. Abraham has his chief steward take an oath. Now the reader is not told who the eldest servant is; however, the reader can make an assumption as to whom the eldest servant is and that is Eliezer of Damascus by the follow:

Genesis 15:2

> And Abram said, LORD God, what wilt thou give me, seeing I go childless, and the steward of my house is this Eliezer of Damascus?

Put, I pray thee, thy hand under my thigh: This method of taking an oath is found only in two instances in scripture in this passage:

Genesis 47:29

> And the time drew nigh that Israel must die: and he called his son Joseph, and said unto him, If now I have found grace in thy sight, put, I pray thee, thy hand under my thigh, and deal kindly and truly with me; bury me not, I pray thee, in Egypt:

According to the biblical idioms, children are said to issue from the thigh or loins of their father, thus a euphemism for the procreative organ:

Genesis 46:26

> All the souls that came with Jacob into Egypt, which came out of his loins, besides Jacob's sons' wives, all the souls were threescore and six;

Therefore, the formality of placing the hand upon or under the thigh was taken to signify that if the oath were violated, the children who came forth or may in the future would avenge the act of disloyalty.[166] However, John Calvin states, "It either signifies subjection or for a further mystery of the covenant of circumcision, or rather of Christ the promised seed, who was to come out of Abraham's loins or thigh."[167] A third voice, that of J. Vernon McGee, states, "The method in that day was for a man to put his hand under the thigh of the man to whom he was going to make an oath."[168] The point he

---

166   . *The Pentateuch and Haftorahs*, edited by Dr. J. H. Hertz (1960), page 82; Publisher: The Soncino Press Limited, 123 Ditmas Avenue, Brooklyn, New York 11218.

167   .Calvin's Commentary, Volume 2 – Genesis (2003), page 12; Publisher: Baker Books, P. O. Box 6287, Grand rapids, Mi 49516-6287.

168   . *Thru The Bible*, volume 1, page 97.

is making, in that day they did not raise their right hand and have the left hand on the Holy Bible, and do solemnly swear. They did not have the Bible!

Taking Thigh Oath[169]

Swear by the LORD, the God of heaven, and the God of the earth: The oath was by Jehovah, God of heaven and earth, as the God who rules in heaven and on earth, not by Elohim; for this was no ordinary oath, but one of great importance in relation to the kingdom of God.[170] This phraseology within the patriarchal narrative is only found here, but will be commonly used in later scripture.

The daughters of the Canaanites: God had told Abraham that his seed would possess this land and the command to marry within the redeemed of God is to be maintained, not only in biblical times, but for the believers of this modern world. Scripture makes this clear:

---

169   . http://efoj.files.wordpress.com/2011/01/thigh-oath-gustave-dore.jpg.

170   . Commentary on the Old Testament; by C. F. Keil and F. Delitzsch, Volume 1, The Pentateuch, page 164 (Third Printing – 2011); Hendrickson Publishers Marketing, LCC, P. O. Box 3473, Peabody, Massachusetts 01961-3473.

Deuteronomy 7:3–4

3. Neither shalt thou make marriages with them; thy daughter thou shalt not give unto his son, nor his daughter shalt thou take unto thy son.

4. For they will turn away thy son from following me, that they may serve other gods: so will the anger of the LORD be kindled against you, and destroy thee suddenly.

1 Kings 11:4

For it came to pass, when Solomon was old, that his wives turned away his heart after other gods: and his heart was not perfect with the LORD his God, as was the heart of David his father.

2 Corinthians 6:14–15

14. Be ye not unequally yoked together with unbelievers: for what fellowship hath righteousness with unrighteousness? and what communion hath light with darkness?

15. And what concord hath Christ with Belial? or what part hath he that believeth with an infidel?

Take a wife unto my son Isaac: Abraham tells his trusted servant he is to return to the city of Nahor and obtain a wife for Isaac. The journey was several hundred miles, and he was not to take Isaac with him. In verses 6 and 7, Abraham provides the reason, Isaac is of this land and he is to remain on the land of promise. God shall send His angel before you to prepare the way and you will bring back a wife for Isaac.

If the woman is not willing to follow: Abraham states that Eliezer is released from the oath if no woman would come, but he is not to take Isaac back under any circumstance this is their land and home, thus sayth the Lord God.

ELIEZER'S PRAYER
Genesis 24:10–14

10. And the servant took ten camels of the camels of his master, and departed; for all the goods of his master were in his hand: and he rose, and went to Mesopotamia, unto the city of Nahor.

11. *And he made his camels to kneel down without the city by a well of water at the time of the evening, even the time that women go out to draw water.*

12. *And he said O LORD God of my master Abraham, I pray thee, send me good speed this day, and shew kindness unto my master Abraham.*

13. *Behold, I stand here by the well of water; and the daughters of the men of the city come out to draw water:*

14. *And let it come to pass, that the damsel to whom I shall say, Let down thy pitcher, I pray thee, that I may drink; and she shall say, Drink, and I will give thy camels drink also: let the same be she that thou hast appointed for thy servant Isaac; and thereby shall I know that thou hast shewed kindness unto my master.*

Eliezer took ten camels of the camels; this is an indication of the wealth of Abraham, and that there are herdsman accompanying him. They arose and went to Nahor or Haran the Mesopotamia city.

Note:

    Mesopotamia is what we know as Iraq and Syrian. Mesopotamia is Greek mean the land between the waters, the area of the Tigris and Euphrates.

Having arrived, he caused the camels to keen at the well. This is a wise thing to do for it was the young maiden's task to fetch the water for the family's needs. He now prays for guidance. This is the first instance of requesting God to provide a specific action of God to know what one should do; another example found in:

Judges 6:36–37

36. And Gideon said unto God, If thou wilt save Israel by mine hand, as thou hast said,

37. Behold, I will put a fleece of wool in the floor; and if the dew be on the fleece only, and it be dry upon all the earth beside, then shall I know that thou wilt save Israel by mine hand, as thou hast said.

38. And it was so: for he rose up early on the morrow, and thrust the fleece together, and wringed the dew out of the fleece, a bowl full of water.

It is from these verses we get the expression "fleece it out" when we need to make an important decision. It is always best to seek our God's direction in all matters.

Eliezer's fleece is that the maiden shall give him drink and shall offer to water his camels also. If this occurs, he has made the correct choice, and then he must speak to male family member to let her become Mrs. Isaac.

MEETING AT THE WELL
Genesis 24:15–27

15. *And it came to pass, before he had done speaking, that, behold, Rebekah came out, who was born to Bethuel, son of Milcah, the wife of Nahor, Abraham's brother, with her pitcher upon her shoulder.*

16. *And the damsel was very fair to look upon, a virgin, neither had any man known her: and she went down to the well, and filled her pitcher, and came up.*

17. *And the servant ran to meet her, and said, Let me, I pray thee, drink a little water of thy pitcher.*

18. *And she said, Drink, my lord: and she hasted, and let down her pitcher upon her hand, and gave him drink.*

19. *And when she had done giving him drink, she said, I will draw water for thy camels also, until they have done drinking.*

20. *And she hasted, and emptied her pitcher into the trough, and ran again unto the well to draw water, and drew for all his camels.*

21. *And the man wondering at her held his peace, to wit whether the LORD had made his journey prosperous or not.*

22. *And it came to pass, as the camels had done drinking, that the man took a golden earring of half a shekel weight, and two bracelets for her hands of ten shekels weight of gold;*

23. *And said, Whose daughter art thou? tell me, I pray thee: is there room in thy father's house for us to lodge in?*

24. *And she said unto him, I am the daughter of Bethuel the son of Milcah, which she bare unto Nahor.*

25. *She said moreover unto him, We have both straw and provender enough, and room to lodge in.*

26. *And the man bowed down his head, and worshipped the LORD.*

27. *And he said, Blessed be the LORD God of my master Abraham, who hath not left destitute my master of his mercy and his truth: I being in the way, the LORD led me to the house of my master's brethren.*

Abrahams Servant Meets Rebecca[171]

Before Eliezer had finished his prayer, God had the situation in control and the damsel Rebekah appeared. As Eliezer prayed for guidance, parents should be in prayer for their children's spouse that they not be unequally yoked with a non-believer.

Very fair to look upon: The reader is given a description of Rebekah; she possesses physical beauty as well as goodness of heart.. When Eliezer asks for a drink of water, she does not hesitate; although he is a stranger, she initiates the watering of his camels, and one may assume, she provided drink for the men that accompanied him.

Eliezer is amazed at her and wonders is this the damsel for Isaac. When she has completed the task of watering the animals, he presents her with gold earrings of ½ a shekel weight, approximately 5.25 grams or ¼ ounce, and two bracelets of 10 shekel weight, approximately 100 grams or 5 ounces. These gifts where of gratitude and a means of obtaining favor.[172]

Eliezer then has two questions for her: (1) whose daughter is she, and (2) can they lodge in her father's house. Her responses that she is of Abraham's brother and there is not only room for them, but also feed for his animals. At this Eliezer worships the Almighty for he sees the hand of God at work.

I being in the way: This statement is not a negative, but rather a positive, meaning he is walking with the Lord God and God has guided him there to do Abraham's biding. This a great phrase, to be in the will of God is a marvelous feeling. A person must be willing, for God will lead those who seek the righteousness of Christ Jesus through His work at Calvary. Scripture makes it clear:

John 14:6

> Jesus saith unto him, I am the way, the truth, and the life: no man cometh unto the Father, but by me.

REACTION OF LABAN
Genesis 24:28–33

28. *And the damsel ran, and told them of her mother's house these things.*
29. *And Rebekah had a brother, and his name was Laban: and Laban ran out unto the man, unto the well.*
30. *And it came to pass, when he saw the earring and bracelets upon his sister's hands, and when he heard the words of Rebekah his sister, saying, Thus spake the man unto me; that he came unto the man; and, behold, he stood by the camels at the well.*
31. *And he said, Come in, thou blessed of the LORD; wherefore standest thou without? for I have prepared the house, and room for the camels.*

---

172 . *The Pentateuch and Haftorahs*, page 84.

32. And the man came into the house: and he ungirded his camels, and gave straw and provender for the camels, and water to wash his feet, and the men's feet that were with him.

33. And there was set meat before him to eat: but he said, I will not eat, until I have told mine errand. And he said, Speak on.

The reader should note how Rebekah's brother reacts. Laban hearing and seeing the gifts of the stranger makes a beeline to the well and to Eliezer. It would appear that he is a materialist, as will become clear later in the study. He says to Eliezer, "*Come in, thou blessed of the LORD; wherefore standest thou without? for I have prepared the house, and room for the camels.*" Eliezer and his men are as honor guest, as Laban unloaded the camels and feed them and washed the feed of Eliezer and his men, and put out a meat to eat.

Note:

The normal diet consisted of vegetables and fruits; the eating of meat was reserved for banquets and feasts.[173]

Even today on the Arabia Peninsula, the Bedouin (desert nomads) diet consist of dates, goat or camel cheese, and milk. Meat is eaten, but at banquets and feast day, normally religious occasion, or weddings.

Eliezer refuses to eat until he explains his mission. Laban thus said speak.

THE MISSION OF ELIEZER
Genesis 24:34–49

34. And he said, I am Abraham's servant.

35. And the LORD hath blessed my master greatly; and he is become great: and he hath given him flocks, and herds, and silver, and gold, and menservants, and maidservants, and camels, and asses.

36. And Sarah my master's wife bare a son to my master when she was old: and unto him hath he given all that he hath.

---

173 . *Illustrated Manners and Customs of the Bible* (1980), Editors: J. I. Packer & M. C. Tenney; page 470; Publisher: Thomas Nelson Inc, Nashville, Tennessee.

37. *And my master made me swear, saying, Thou shalt not take a wife to my son of the daughters of the Canaanites, in whose land I dwell:*

38. *But thou shalt go unto my father's house, and to my kindred, and take a wife unto my son.*

39. *And I said unto my master, Peradventure the woman will not follow me.*

40. *And he said unto me, The LORD, before whom I walk, will send his angel with thee, and prosper thy way; and thou shalt take a wife for my son of my kindred, and of my father's house:*

41. *Then shalt thou be clear from this my oath, when thou comest to my kindred; and if they give not thee one, thou shalt be clear from my oath.*

42. *And I came this day unto the well, and said, O LORD God of my master Abraham, if now thou do prosper my way which I go:*

43. *Behold, I stand by the well of water; and it shall come to pass, that when the virgin cometh forth to draw water, and I say to her, Give me, I pray thee, a little water of thy pitcher to drink;*

44. *And she say to me, Both drink thou, and I will also draw for thy camels: let the same be the woman whom the LORD hath appointed out for my master's son.*

45. *And before I had done speaking in mine heart, behold, Rebekah came forth with her pitcher on her shoulder; and she went down unto the well, and drew water: and I said unto her, Let me drink, I pray thee.*

46. *And she made haste, and let down her pitcher from her shoulder, and said, Drink, and I will give thy camels drink also: so I drank, and she made the camels drink also.*

47. *And I asked her, and said, Whose daughter art thou? And she said, the daughter of Bethuel, Nahor's son, whom Milcah bare unto him: and I put the earring upon her face, and the bracelets upon her hands.*

48. *And I bowed down my head, and worshipped the LORD, and blessed the LORD God of my master Abraham, which had led me in the right way to take my master's brother's daughter unto his son.*

49. *And now if ye will deal kindly and truly with my master, tell me: and if not, tell me; that I may turn to the right hand, or to the left.*

Eliezer now begins to recite his errand by telling them, "*I am Abraham's servant,*" and the wealth of Uncle Abraham, and that it will pass into the hands of Isaac. This followed, by a discourse of his mission, in effect to secure a wife for Isaac. He further describes his prayer at the well to fleece out who he should approach and the specific of the fleece.

He relates how Rebekah reacted in the fulfilling of his prayer, and glory be to God when she related her lineage, that she was a kinsman of his master Abraham. Eliezer then worshiped the Lord God.

With the explanation now completed, Eliezer wants to know their answer: shall he return with a bride, or shall he go away empty handed?

The ball is how in the court of Laban and Bethuel: (1) they are going to consent to the evident providential leading of God. (2) If not, he will make the offer to someone else. If they say no, they will have evidenced faithlessness to God and kin and would have lost the best possible dowry for the girl.[174]

ELIEZER HAS OBTAINED CONSENT
Genesis 24:50–61

50. *Then Laban and Bethuel answered and said, The thing proceedeth from the LORD: we cannot speak unto thee bad or good.*

51. *Behold, Rebekah is before thee, take her, and go, and let her be thy master's son's wife, as the LORD hath spoken.*

52. *And it came to pass, that, when Abraham's servant heard their words, he worshipped the LORD, bowing himself to the earth.*

53. *And the servant brought forth jewels of silver, and jewels of gold, and raiment, and gave them to Rebekah: he gave also to her brother and to her mother precious things.*

54. *And they did eat and drink, he and the men that were with him, and tarried all night; and they rose up in the morning, and he said, Send me away unto my master.*

55. *And her brother and her mother said, Let the damsel abide with us a few days, at the least ten; after that she shall go.*

56. *And he said unto them, Hinder me not, seeing the LORD hath prospered my way; send me away that I may go to my master.*

57. *And they said, We will call the damsel, and enquire at her mouth.*

58. *And they called Rebekah, and said unto her, Wilt thou go with this man? And she said, I will go.*

---

174   & 8. The Broadman Bible Commentary, volume 1, page 196.

> 59. *And they sent away Rebekah their sister, and her nurse, and Abraham's servant, and his men.*
>
> 60. *And they blessed Rebekah, and said unto her, Thou art our sister, be thou the mother of thousands of millions, and let thy seed possess the gate of those which hate them.*
>
> 61. *And Rebekah arose, and her damsels, and they rode upon the camels, and followed the man: and the servant took Rebekah, and went his way.*

Laban and Bethuel said this is of God; "Rebekah is yours." When Eliezer heard this, he rejoiced in the Lord God and worshiped the "Great I Am." After worshipping God and giving thanks, he brought forth jewelry of gold and silver, and fine clothing for Rebekah. He did the same for her brother and mother, the "*mohar*" or compensation for her loss to the family. Clyde T. Francisco makes this observation.[175]

There is considerable evidence that Bethuel, Rebekah's father, was not alive at this time. Under examination (1) Verse 28, Rebekah runs to her mother's house not her father's house. (2) Verse 53, Eliezer gave gifts to Rebekah's brother and mother. (3) Verse 55, her mother and brother spoke for Rebekah. (4) Verse 50, Laban is mentioned before the father, which is not customary.

These events are typical for when the brother acted in the place of a dead or absent father. There are two possibilities: (1) the name Bethuel comes into verse 50 by scribal error, or (2) the man was completely overshadowed by an ambitious son and dominating wife.

Their business now completed, Eliezer and his men did feast and remained for the night. Raising in the morning, Eliezer requested they send him back to Abraham, post haste, but they want them to remain ten days to say good-bye to Rebekah, for they loathe the sudden departure of their daughter, as they might never see again.

Enquire at her mouth: The rabbis take it to mean as to whether she wishes to follow Eliezer, and deduce from this text the rule that a woman cannot legally be given in marriage without her consent.[176] They sent for her and ask would she go with Eliezer, and she replied "I will go." So she and her nurse (her name was Deborah, see below) departed following the blessing:

175
176   . *The Pentateuch and Haftorahs*, page 87.

Genesis 24:60

> And they blessed Rebekah, and said unto her, Thou art our sister, be thou the mother of thousands of millions, and let thy seed possess the gate of those which hate them.

Genesis 35:8

> But Deborah Rebekah's nurse died, and she was buried beneath Bethel under an oak: and the name of it was called Allonbachuth.

Verse 61 states that Rebekah, and her damsels took their position in the rear of this caravan, heading south into Canaan. The Position at the rear is the customary place for woman in Middle East, even today. Woman are relegated to the back of the bus, and there are just a few seats.

This was long and hard trek, I can imagine Rebekah every night asking about Isaac. Can you not see them around the fire, Rebekah asking question after question, and Eliezer gently telling her over and over the history of Isaac. What he look like, the story of the sacrifice and the appearance of the ram, of his miraculous birth—his mother ninety years of age and his father a hundred years of age. Can you not hear her, come on Eliezer tell me again.[177]

CONSUMMATION OF MARRIAGE
Genesis 24:62–67

> 62. *And Isaac came from the way of the well Lahairoi; for he dwelt in the south country.*
>
> 63. *And Isaac went out to meditate in the field at the eventide: and he lifted up his eyes, and saw, and, behold, the camels were coming.*
>
> 64. *And Rebekah lifted up her eyes, and when she saw Isaac, she lighted off the camel.*
>
> 65. *For she had said unto the servant, What man is this that walketh in the field to meet us? And the servant had said, It is my master: therefore she took a vail, and covered herself.*
>
> 66. *And the servant told Isaac all things that he had done.*
>
> 67. *And Isaac brought her into his mother Sarah's tent, and took Rebekah, and she became his wife; and he loved her: and Isaac was comforted after his mother's death.*

---

177   . *Thru The Bible*, page 104.

To meditate: The rabbinical scholars understand this to mean pray, and declared that Isaac instituted the Afternoon Service; as Abraham instituted the Morning Service:

Genesis 19:27

And Abraham gat up early in the morning to the place where he stood before the LORD.

Jacob later will institute the Evening Service as deduced from:

Genesis 28:11

And he lighted upon a certain place, and tarried there all night, because the sun was set; and he took of the stones of that place, and put them for his pillows, and lay down in that place to sleep.

Rebekah dismounted as a sign of respect to the person coming to meet them, and once she knew who it was, she covered her face; although he was her betrothed, etiquette require she cover up.

Once Eliezer filled Isaac in and made the introduction, Isaac brought Rebekah into his mother's tent. By bring her into what was Sarah tent, he installed Rebekah as mistress of the household. The word *order* is just backward by today's standards; it should be courtship, love, marriage, and lastly take. However, by today's standards, they would not have got married. The order may be backward; however, the marriage lasted a lifetime. The older view emphasizes the life-long devotion and affection after marriage.[178]

Isaac was comforted after his mother's death: The explanation by the rabbinical scholars is that upon the death of Sarah the blessing, which attended the household of the patriarch, ended; but when Rebekah came into the tent, the restoration began. Once again the Sabbath lamp was illuminated in the patriarch's home and Rebekah continue the other religious rites which Sarah had initiated.[179]

---

178 . *The Pentateuch and Haftorahs*, page 87.
179 . *The Pentateuch and Haftorahs*, page 87.

THE DEATH OF ABRAHAM
Genesis 25

Isaac prepares for his burial[180]

180 . www.visualbiblealive.com/image-bin/Public/110/04/110_04_0021_BiblePaintings_prev.jpg.

CHAPTER OVERVIEW

This chapter is packed with information; there is the marriage and death of Abraham, the birth of twins to Isaac and Rebekah, an account of Ishmael's descendants, and the selling of the birthright.

Chapter 25 is not arranged in chronological order with regard to the material covered. Some scholars find it difficult to believe Abraham at age 140 is virile enough to father the family described in verses 1thur 4;[181] however, they are applying man's logic, not God's. When God prepared Sarah to conceive and bear Isaac, as well as rear him, God also prepare Abraham as attested by this chapter.

These skeptics say that Keturah was Abraham's concubine as stated in:

1 Chronicles 1:32
> Now the sons of <u>Keturah, Abraham's concubine</u>: she bare Zimran, and Jokshan, and Medan, and Midian, and Ishbak, and Shuah. And the sons of Jokshan; Sheba, and Dedan.

Of course it is possible that Keturah was his concubine all along and following the death of Sarah was then elevated to wife of the patriarch. However, these passages indicate Abraham lived another thirty-five years and therefore could have reared another family.

The chronology does appear out of order, because Abraham lived for another fifteen years following the birth of Jacob and Esau, but the chapter sequence would indicate he died before they were born.

CHAPTER STRUCTURE

- Abraham Takes a Wife (1–4)
- Inheritance of the heirs (5–6)
- Death and burial of Abraham (7–10)
- An Account of Ishmael (12–18)
- An Account of Isaac (11, 19–24)

---

181   . The Broadman Bible Commentary, Volume 1, page 197.

- The birth of Isaac's twins (25–28)
- Selling of the birthright (29–34)

ABRAHAM TAKES A WIFE
Genesis 25:1–4

1. *Then again Abraham took a wife, and her name was Keturah.*
2. *And she bare him Zimran, and Jokshan, and Medan, and Midian, and Ishbak, and Shuah.*
3. *And Jokshan begat Sheba, and Dedan. And the sons of Dedan were Asshurim, and Letushim, and Leummim.*
4. *And the sons of Midian; Ephah, and Epher, and Hanoch, and Abidah, and Eldaah. All these were the children of Keturah.*

The name Keturah means "the perfumed one," and very likely she of the Arabian tribe of Ketura. This tribe is located on the north-eastern boarder of Palestine. Very little is known of the descendants of this union[182].

Shuah is an ancestor of Bildad:

Job 2:11
> Now when Job's three friends heard of all this evil that was come upon him, they came every one from his own place; Eliphaz the Temanite, and <u>Bildad the Shuhite</u>, and Zophar the Naamathite: for they had made an appointment together to come to mourn with him and to comfort him.

The Kenites were a Midianite tribe, whom Jethro was a member:

Numbers 10:29
> And Moses said unto Hobab, <u>the son of Raguel the Midianite, Moses' father in law</u>, We are journeying unto the place of which the LORD said, I will give it you: come thou with us, and we will do thee good: for the LORD hath spoken good concerning Israel.

---

182 . The Broadman Bible Commentary, volume 1, page 198.

Judges 1:16

> And the <u>children of the Kenite, Moses' father in law</u>, went up out of the city of palm trees with the children of Judah into the wilderness of Judah, which lieth in the south of Arad; and they went and dwelt among the people.

From Dedan came the Dedanim or Dedanites, spoken of with the Arabians in:

Isaiah 21:13

> The burden upon Arabia. In the forest in Arabia shall ye lodge , O ye travelling companies of Dedanim.

The posterity of Sheba are the same the Sabeans who inhabited at the entrance of Arabia Felix:[183,184]

Job 1:15

> And the Sabeans fell upon them, and took them away ; yea, they have slain the servants with the edge of the sword; and I only am escaped alone to tell thee.

Ephah is mentioned along with Midian in:[185]

Isaiah 60:6

> The multitude of camels shall cover thee, the dromedaries of Midian and Ephah; all they from Sheba shall come: they shall bring gold and incense; and they shall shew forth the praises of the LORD.

---

183   . John Gill's Exposition of the Bible, on line provided the info of the descendants of Abraham & Keturah; http://www.ewordtoday.com/comments/genesis/gill/genesis25.htm.

184   184. John Gill's Exposition of the Bible, on line provided the info of the descendants of Abraham & Keturah; http://www.ewordtoday.com/comments/genesis/gill/genesis25.htm.

185   . John Gill's Exposition of the Bible, on line provided the info of the descendants of Abraham & Keturah; http://www.ewordtoday.com/comments/genesis/gill/genesis25.htm.

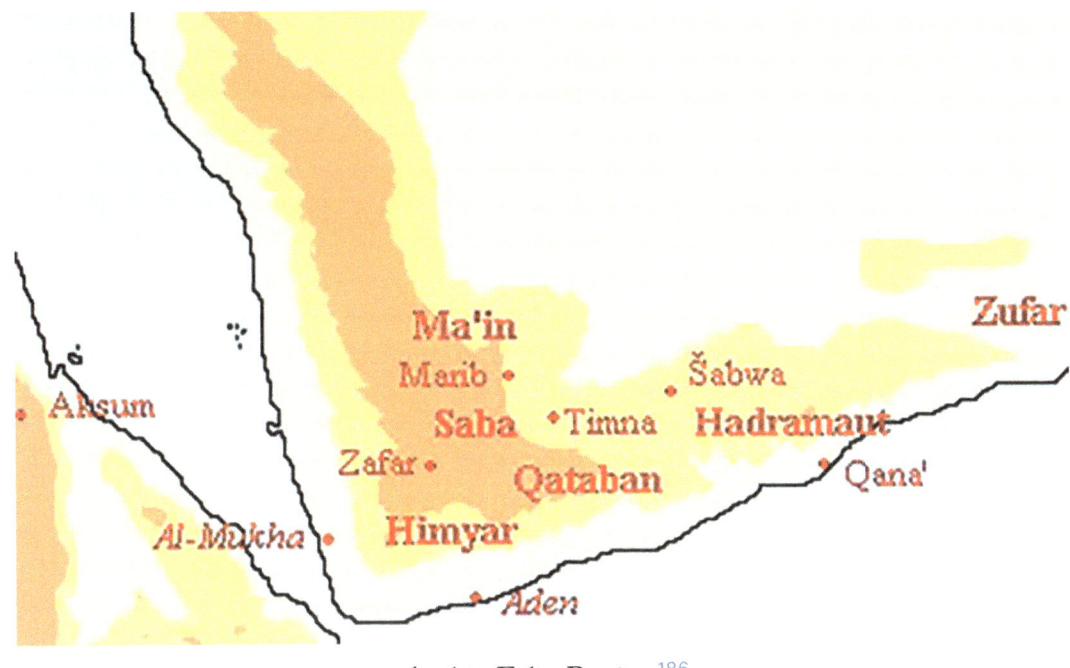

Arabia Felix Region[186]

The region referred to as Arabia Felix is the southwestern corner of the Arabia Peninsula known as Yemen. The descendants of the union of Abraham and Keturah are scatter across the Arabia Peninsula. The term "Happy Arabia" is a translation of the Latin "Arabia felix." *Felix* means "happy, fortunate, blessed."[187]

The southwestern corner of the peninsula, enjoying more rainfall, is greener than the rest of the peninsula and has long enjoyed more productive fields. The high peaks

and slopes are capable of supporting significant vegetation and riverbeds called wadis help make other soil fertile. In 26 BC, Aelius Gallus under Augustus's order led a military expedition to Arabia Felix which ended in the utter defeat of Roman troops. Part of what led to Arabia Felix's wealth and importance to the ancient world was its near monopoly of the trade in cinnamon and spices, both its native products and imports from India and the Horn of Africa.[188]

Arabian Peninsula, Courtesy NASA

---

186   . http://www.livius.org/ap-ark/arabia/arabia.html.
187   & 9. http://en.wikipedia.org/wiki/Arabia_Felix.
188

Abraham				
Wife / Concubine	Children	Grandchildren	Great-Grandchildren	
Keturah	Zimran			
	Jokshan	Sheba		
		Dedan	Asshurim	
			Letushim	
			Leummim	
	Medan			
	Midian	Ephah		
		Epher		
		Hanoch		
		Abidah		
		Eldaah		
	Ishbak			
	Shuah			

Descendants of Abraham and Keturah

The above table is children, grandchildren, great-grandchildren of Keturah and Abraham. These six sons, in whom the promise made to Abraham concerning the great increase of his posterity, was in part fulfilled.

INHERITANCE OF THE HEIRS
Genesis 25:5–6

5. *And Abraham gave all that he had unto Isaac.*
6. *But unto the sons of the concubines, which Abraham had, Abraham gave gifts, and sent them away from Isaac his son, while he yet lived, eastward, unto the east country.*

Not only did Isaac inherit the land God had promise Abraham, but as the son of promise Isaac was recipient of Abraham's estate. He gave portions to the rest of his children, both to Ishmael, though at first he was sent empty away, and to his sons by Keturah. It was justice to provide for them; parents that do not imitate him in this are worse than infidels. It was prudence to settle them in places distant from Isaac that they might not pretend to divide the inheritance with him, nor be in any way a care or expense to him. Observe, He did this *while he yet lived,* lest it should not be done, or not so well done, afterwards. Note, in many cases it is wisdom for men to make their own hands their executors, and what they find to do it while they live, as far as they can. These *sons of the concubines* were sent into the country that lay east from Canaan, and their posterity were called *the children of the east,* famous for their numbers:[189]

Judges 6:5–6, 33

5. For they came up with their cattle and their tents, and they came as grasshoppers for multitude; for both they and their camels were without number: and they entered into the land to destroy it.

6. And Israel was greatly impoverished because of the Midianites; and the children of Israel cried unto the LORD.

33. Then all the Midianites and the Amalekites and the children of the east were gathered together, and went over, and pitched in the valley of Jezreel.

Their great increase was the fruit of the promise made to Abraham, that God would multiply his seed. God, in dispensing his blessings, does as Abraham did; common blessings he gives to the children of this world, as to the sons of the bond-woman, but covenant-blessings he reserves for the heirs of promise. All that he has is theirs, for they are his Isaacs, from whom the rest shall be forever separated.[190]

DEATH AND BURIAL OF ABRAHAM
Genesis 25:7–10

7. *And these are the days of the years of Abraham's life which he lived, an hundred threescore and fifteen years.*

8. *Then Abraham gave up the ghost, and died in a good old age, an old man, and full of years; and was gathered to his people.*

9. *And his sons Isaac and Ishmael buried him in the cave of Machpelah, in the field of Ephron the son of Zohar the Hittite, which is before Mamre;*

---

189 & 11. Matthew Henry's Commentary; volume 1, page.
190 12. John Gill's Exposition of the Entire Bible;
  http://www.ewordtoday.com/comments/genesis/gill/genesis25.htm.

> *10. The field which Abraham purchased of the sons of Heth: there was Abraham buried, and Sarah his wife.*

Abraham was 175 years when he died; Isaac was seventy-five years of age, for he was born when Abraham was a hundred years old. Jacob and Esau are how fifteen years of age as they were born when Isaac was sixty years of age:

Genesis 25:26
> And after that came his brother out, and his hand took hold on Esau's heel; and his name was called Jacob: and Isaac was threescore years old when she bare them.

Ishmael is approximately eighty-nine years old at the time of Abraham's death. Abraham was seventy-five years old when he went from Haran into the land of Canaan:

Genesis 12:4
> So Abram departed, as the LORD had spoken unto him; and Lot went with him: and Abram was seventy and five years old when he departed out of Haran.

Therefore, Abraham had been sojourner in the land of Canaan for hundred years.[191]

Died in a good old age, an old man, and full of years: It is obvious, Abraham thus died of old age, not illness, just the natural cause of a body completely used up and wore out. One can assume a heart attack, as a servant of God; his death was quick and easy.

Isaac and Ishmael buried him: At the death of their father, their differences have been reconciled, at least long enough to bury their father. Their mothers may have understood the importance of the birthright and later they themselves came to understand, as evident by the ongoing conflict within the Mideast. The assumption is that Abraham did provide for Ishmael by verses 6 of this chapter.

---

191   . John Gill's Exposition of the Entire Bible; http://www.ewordtoday.com/comments/genesis/gill/genesis25.htm.

The field and cave He had purchased from the sons of Heth is the final resting place of Abraham. His two eldest son laid him to rest beside his beloved Sarah in the mausoleum of the patriarchs.

AN ACCOUNT OF ISHMAEL
Genesis 25:12–18

12. *Now these are the generations of Ishmael, Abraham's son, whom Hagar the Egyptian, Sarah's handmaid, bare unto Abraham:*

13. *And these are the names of the sons of Ishmael, by their names, according to their generations: the firstborn of Ishmael, Nebajoth; and Kedar, and Adbeel, and Mibsam,*

14. *And Mishma, and Dumah, and Massa,*

15. *Hadar, and Tema, Jetur, Naphish, and Kedemah:*

16. *These are the sons of Ishmael, and these are their names, by their towns, and by their castles; twelve princes according to their nations.*

17. *And these are the years of the life of Ishmael, an hundred and thirty and seven years: and he gave up the ghost and died; and was gathered unto his people.*

18. *And they dwelt from Havilah unto Shur, that is before Egypt, as thou goest toward Assyria: and he died in the presence of all his brethren.*

The genealogy of Ishmael's posterity, and which is given to show that the Lord was not unmindful of his promise made to Abraham, concerning the multiplication of his seed:[192]

Genesis 16

10. And the angel of the LORD said unto her, I will multiply thy seed exceedingly, that it shall not be numbered for multitude.

11. And the angel of the LORD said unto her, Behold, thou art with child, and shalt bear a son, and shalt call his name Ishmael; because the LORD hath heard thy affliction.

See chapter 17 for accounting of the sons of Ishmael, and where they dwelt. Ishmael pass on at 137 years of age and they laid him to rest with his brethren.

---

192   . John Gill's Exposition of the Entire Bible; http://www.ewordtoday.com/comments/genesis/gill/genesis25.htm.

AN ACCOUNT OF ISAAC
Genesis 25:11, 19–24

19. And it came to pass after the death of Abraham, that God blessed his son Isaac; and Isaac dwelt by the well Lahairoi.

20. And these are the generations of Isaac, Abraham's son: Abraham begat Isaac:

21. And Isaac was forty years old when he took Rebekah to wife, the daughter of Bethuel the Syrian of Padanaram, the sister to Laban the Syrian.

22. And Isaac intreated the LORD for his wife, because she was barren: and the LORD was intreated of him, and Rebekah his wife conceived.

23. And the children struggled together within her; and she said, If it be so, why am I thus? And she went to enquire of the LORD.

24. And the LORD said unto her, Two nations are in thy womb, and two manner of people shall be separated from thy bowels; and the one people shall be stronger than the other people; and the elder shall serve the younger.

25. And when her days to be delivered were fulfilled, behold, there were twins in her womb.

Both with spiritual and temporal blessings; showing hereby, that, though Abraham was dead, God was not unmindful of His covenant, which should be established with Isaac:

Genesis 17:19

And God said, Sarah thy wife shall bear thee a son indeed; and thou shalt call his name Isaac: and I will establish my covenant with him for an everlasting covenant, and with his seed after him.

Isaac dwelt by the well Lahairoi: Which is near the wilderness of Beersheba and Paran, where Ishmael dwelt, so that they were not far from one another:

Genesis 16:14

Wherefore the well was called Beerlahairoi ; behold, it is between Kadesh and Bered.

Isaac was married to Rebekah at forty years old and then waited twenty years for her to conceive and bear him son, but only after he sought the help of God.

The children struggled together within her: It was some time before her delivery and was not a common and ordinary motion felt by women in such circumstances. It was extraordinary one, because the two children in her fought with each other: (1) was it for mastery, (2) who would be first before the proper time. This caused Rebekah great uneasiness of mind, but pain of body. As this is not normal, she beseeched the Almighty God and was told there are two nations struggling within her.

Psalm 73:17
  Until I went into the sanctuary of God; then understood I their end

The two nations, Esau the elder the father of the Edomites, and Jacob would be the father of the twelve tribes of the Israelites. And as her time came, she delivered twins and the elder will serve the younger, which is exactly what happened.[193]

THE BIRTH OF ISAAC'S TWINS
Genesis 25:25–28

26. *And the first came out red, all over like an hairy garment; and they called his name Esau.*
27. *And after that came his brother out, and his hand took hold on Esau's heel; and his name was called Jacob: and Isaac was threescore years old when she bare them.*
28. *And the boys grew: and Esau was a cunning hunter, a man of the field; and Jacob was a plain man, dwelling in tents.*
29. *And Isaac loved Esau, because he did eat of his venison: but Rebekah loved Jacob.*

The boys grew in stature, became strong and fit for business, and betook themselves to different employments:

(1) Esau was a cunning hunter, a man of the field, whose business lay in tilling and sowing it. Ranging about the field and hunt after beasts and birds, in which he was very expert, and contrived traps and snares to catch them in. This life was most agreeable to his temper and disposition, being active, fierce, and cruel. He was also a hunter and slayer of men, Nimrod and Henoch his son, per the rabbinical scholars.

---

193 . John Gill's Exposition of the Entire Bible; http://www.ewordtoday.com/comments/genesis/gill/genesis25.htm.

(2) Jacob was a plain man; an honest man, whose heart and tongue went together. A quiet man that gave no disturbance to others; a godly man, sincere, upright, and perfect that had the truth of grace and holiness in him. Dwelling in tents; keeping at home and attending the business of the family. His pastoral life, being a shepherd, he dwelt in tents, which could be removed from place to place for the convenience of pasturage.[194]

Their parents had their favor's, Esau was Isaac and Jacob was his mother. This is mainly because of the personalities they possessed.

SELLING OF THE BIRTHRIGHT
Genesis 25:29–34

> 30. *And Jacob sod pottage: and Esau came from the field, and he was faint:*
> 31. *And Esau said to Jacob, Feed me, I pray thee, with that same red pottage; for I am faint: therefore was his name called Edom.*
> 32. *And Jacob said, Sell me this day thy birthright.*
> 33. *And Esau said, Behold, I am at the point to die: and what profit shall this birthright do to me?*
> 34. *And Jacob said, Swear to me this day; and he swear unto him: and he sold his birthright unto Jacob.*
> 35. *Then Jacob gave Esau bread and pottage of lentils; and he did eat and drink, and rose up, and went his way: thus Esau despised his birthright.*

Jacob was far more of a scammer than this brother and con Esau of his birthright for bread and bowl of bean dinner. Because of Esau's disrespect and devaluing of the birthright, God hated Esau and loved Jacob.

Malachi 1:2–3

1. "I have loved you," says the Lord. "Yet you say, 'In what way have You loved us?'
2. Was not Esau Jacob's brother?" Says the Lord. "Yet Jacob I have loved;
3. But Esau I have hated, And laid waste his mountains and his heritage For the jackals of the wilderness."

---

194   . John Gill's Exposition of the Entire Bible; http://www.ewordtoday.com/comments/genesis/gill/genesis25.htm.

Romans 9:10–13

10. And not only this, but when Rebecca also had conceived by one man, even by our father Isaac

11. (for the children not yet being born, nor having done any good or evil, that the purpose of God according to election might stand, not of works but of Him who calls),

12. it was said to her, "The older shall serve the younger."

13. As it is written, "Jacob I have loved, but Esau I have hated."